GEORGE MASON
and the
War for Independence

D1288899

George Mason in 1750. Painted in 1811 by Dominic W. Boudet, after the lost portrait by John Hesselius. *Courtesy of the Virginia Museum of Fine Arts, Richmond, and the Board of Regents of Gunston Hall.*

GEORGE MASON
and the
War for Independence

Robert A. Rutland

Edward M. Riley, *Editor*

Published by the
Virginia Independence Bicentennial Commission
Drawer JF
Williamsburg, Virginia 23185

Commonwealth of Virginia
Virginia Independence Bicentennial Commission

Lewis A. McMurran, Jr., *Chairman*
Hunter B. Andrews, *Vice Chairman*

Fred W. Bateman
Garland Gray
Omer Lee Hirst
John Warren Cooke
W. C. Daniel
Frank E. Mann
Sam E. Pope
John Sears, Jr.

Robert R. Gwathmey III
A. E. Dick Howard
W. Moscoe Huntley
E. M. Hutton
Mrs. Carolyn Moses Lusardi
Mrs. Perry W. Moore
Jack C. Smith
John C. Stephens, Jr.

Parke Rouse, Jr., *Director*
Robert L. Scribner, *Historian*

Committee on Publications
Edward M. Riley,
Chairman

Francis L. Berkeley, Jr.
Alf J. Mapp, Jr.
A. E. Dick Howard

John M. Jennings
William F. Swindler
Louis H. Manarin

George H. Reese

v

To
Lester Cappon

Table of Contents

Chapter I

Politics Along the Potomac

In the life of every great nation there comes a time when good men and great affairs join together, producing an era that blazes across all history. In the history of the United States, that time came at the outset of a venturesome journey into nationhood which we call the American Revolution. All of the colonies-states made a contribution to that struggle, but two stood out—Massachusetts and Virginia. Southern and New England leaders struck the first sparks of revolt and helped fan embers until they were flames. Whether the Old Dominion will ever again see men of the caliber of a Washington, Madison, Jefferson, or George Mason is not certain, but that such giants lived at the same time, were dedicated to the same cause, and worked for the same ends was a coincidence that still causes wonderment. Fortunate is that place whence they sprang, where they were nurtured, and that remained always in their thoughts— Virginia.

Until the shattering experience after 1765, Virginia was only thought of as a convenient retreat for Englishmen of high hopes but low fortunes, for ship captains anxious to profit from lucrative cargoes of slaves or tobacco or lumber, or a place for planters resigned to the quiet isolation of plantation living. But the rush of events after 1765 ended the peaceful prospects, and the Revolution brewing after word of the Boston Port Bill reached Williamsburg drew upon the talents of Virginians who in ordinary times were not prone to favor change.

George Mason of Gunston Hall was such a Virginian. Mason enjoyed the Anglo-American ties that bound his Northern Neck plantation by sentiment to a distant estate in Staffordshire. The identification of Mason's family with the well-being of that English county went back to the 15th century. George Mason, however, was a Virginian whose allegiance was to his family, his friends, and his beloved Virginia. In the mind's eye we can see Mason, standing on the Gunston knoll above the Potomac, and almost feel the inner satisfaction of this self-educated and reserved man whose intellect became a potent weapon in the first and greatest revolution of modern times.

George Mason's place in the hearts of Virginians was firmly fixed from 1776 until the end of the 19th century. Mason's name was always mentioned in the galaxy that included Washington, Jefferson, Madison and Patrick Henry. His statue was placed among the demi-gods on the capitol grounds at Richmond. The eclipse of southern statesmen for several generations ended after World War I, when Mason's contributions to Virginia and the nation were remembered as hotels, high schools, postage stamps, streets and libraries were named or issued in his honor. Increasingly, however, the Virginians who knew of Mason's real work grew fewer, and in the 1970s proud natives who took visitors from out-of-state to his showplace home at Gunston Hall had to do their homework or confess that Mason "had something to do with George Washington."

Indeed, George Mason had many dealings with his distinguished and more active neighbor from Mount Vernon. Yet the lapse of his reputation and attempts at its revival tell us a good deal about the whole process of history. For the truth is that George Mason has been viewed in different ways by different generations, and when we probe into the ambering documents with their faded ink we can learn at least what Mason's contemporaries thought of him. History changes with interpretations and historians, but the judgment of a man's (or woman's) closest associates at the time they lived is a fact beyond dispute. In that light, George Mason stands forth as one of the outstanding men in American Revolution—a Virginian whose pen and mind helped shape the laws and destiny of the thirteen colonies and the nation that was to be.

A few patriots established their reputations early in the struggle and to some degree coasted on their fame. This was true of Samuel Adams, John Hancock, and Patrick Henry. Henry continued to strut on the stage of the Revolution, although he was popular without having taken any courageous stands after 1776. As for talk, there was probably no other man of the period who was more of a spellbinder than Henry, but for those not blinded by his brilliant oratory there was a more responsive audience for Mason.

2

Far from being a stage-strutter, Mason would have liked to avoid even a supporting role in the Revolutionary drama if he could be spared. Mason hated committee haggling, he despised the windy oratory, and after a few days of work in a legislative body he was nearly always irritable and impatient for the familiar lane leading to Gunston Hall. "Mr Mason is a Gentleman of remarkable strong powers, and possess a clear and copious understanding," a fellow delegate at the Federal Convention, William Pierce of Georgia, thus described George Mason. "He is able and convincing in debate, steady and firm in his principles, and undoubtedly one of the best politicians in America." The same observer thought Washington was "the deliverer of his Country," and considered Madison a blend of "the profound politician, with the Scholar." George Mason kept good company. Indeed, one of the marvels of American history is the fact that Washington, Jefferson, Madison, Marshall, and Monroe were all of the generations that flowered between 1773 and the end of the century. Four of the six were not only revolutionary leaders but also served as presidents, and one became more powerful than most presidents when he presided as chief justice for almost nine presidential terms. Of this triumphant group of talent, only one Virginian of stature fended off high office and indeed occasionally appeared to despise public duty. That exception was George Mason. Although Mason's credentials as a Founding Father are of the highest order, Mason was unlike the other Virginians whom destiny handed the reins of power. Mason had known the effect of power from the 1760's onward and vowed that he did not like the sight, smell, or feel of political power. (Our seniority system, so much a part of the American legislative history, would have infuriated Mason, since he thought the only way to keep public men humble was to periodically return them to "that station whence they came".)

Since the point of politics is a delight in the wielding of power, the outcome of simple logic is that Mason was no ordinary politician. He was, rather, "a public man"—an expression that once carried a complimentary meaning, indicating that in fact the person was a servant of the people. Mason distrusted power in the hands of most men, hence his efforts to throttle political power and to make sure that it could not be concentrated too long in any one segment of society.

We hear a good deal about public servants these days, for every government employee is alluded to (during election years, anyway) as "a faithful servant," and bombastic senators tend to think of their

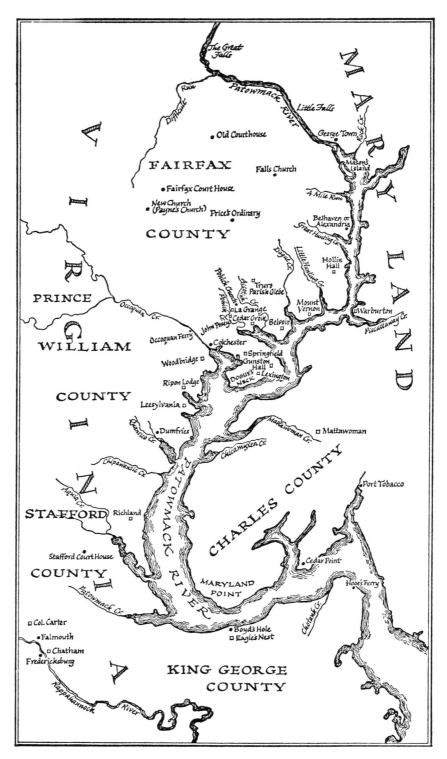

The region of the upper Potomac as George Mason knew it. Placenames and spellings largely conform to those of the Fry-Jefferson map (1755). Locations of plantations (□), and town sites, ferries, and public buildings (•) are approximate.

years in office as time solely devoted to the public good. Voters sometimes have other ideas, but in Mason's time it would have been easy to find scores of Virginians who would readily concede that there were but a handful of public servants in the Commonwealth and that surely George Mason was among them.

Washington reached his station by a single-minded devotion to a military career which he submerged during his later career into a life of the planter and local politician. Jefferson, more the theorist and idealist, studied at the College of William and Mary and cultivated a passionate fondness for books. Madison, an idealist with a streak of practical politician, loved books but tried always to keep one foot on the ground. Mason wanted only to be a successful planter, a good husband, and a worthy father. He read, but not as widely as his younger friends from Monticello and Montpelier, and Gunston Hall rang with the shouts of nine children, so that through most of his life he took to his library only after the duties of his daily life had been attended.

Although Mason usually stood alongside Richard Henry Lee and Patrick Henry in factional battles in Virginia, he was closer to Madison intellectually—a fact that Madison recalled long after the master of Gunston Hall had died. The two had worked together on the Virginia Declaration of Rights, fought the attempt to reestablish a state-supported church, and worked for the interstate harmony that resulted in the Federal Convention of 1787. On the great issues, the two men had always been in unison, and yet they parted company over the Constitution and fought tenaciously but fairly. Thus Madison recalled that despite their differences they always rose above petty politics to view the needs of their country in a broad light. "My private intercourse with him was chiefly on occasional visits to Gunston when journeying to & fro from the North," Madison remembered, "in which his conversations were always a feast to me." Madison's dear friend, Jefferson, rendered a similar judgment when a minor dispute arose a generation after Mason's death. A distant kinsman had sought information regarding claims that a distinguished ancestor was the real author of the Virginia Declaration of Rights, not Mason. When asked to clarify the matter, Jefferson replied that the declaration had indeed been "drawn originally by George Mason, one of our really great men, and of the first order of greatness."

Mason's greatness came to the fore only after England won the great French and Indian War but began to lose the peace that followed. While Virginians were clearing more land to plant larger crops of tobacco, well-fed Englishmen in Whitehall were little concerned about the wretchedness of the London poor. The fact was that the war had cost an enormous sum, the British national debt had climbed to £130 million, and London investors were worried. Their concern was echoed in Parliament, where in time the decision was made to shift some of the costs of the war (and the peacetime army needed to consolidate its gains) to America. The British ministers who made this decision were not evil men, but only hard-headed business men who thought Americans would not balk at paying a three-penny tax on molasses instead of the old six-penny tax that somehow had scarcely ever been collected by lax customs officials. Yet the Sugar Act of 1764 started America down the road to rebellion, and although George Mason had—so far as we know—no great love for molasses or the rum it made, still Mason had a love for one principle that was involved from the time Parliament had passed the unfortunate legislation. He wanted no taxes levied by men in London for collection in America—and in the neat phrase "No Taxation Without Representation" we see the reason Mason and his friends grew restive, then bold, and finally defiant of Mother England.

Strange business, that a tiny quarrel over three pence on a gallon of molasses should start the political volcano that erupted after 1764. But in history the greatest causes often spring from the infinitesimal affairs of men, and only after generations pass can the historians look back and pinpoint the moment when a momentary tremor was a warning unheeded. Surely when George Mason first read of the Sugar Act he was not profoundly shocked. For one thing, the colony chiefly affected by the Sugar Act was Massachusetts, where the sticky stuff was converted into cheap rum for the laboring men, landlubbers, and seafaring crews. At Gunston Hall the refreshments were Madeira, port, cider, tea, coffee, and hardly anything so strong as the potent rum. But there was the principle involved—and when Parliament moved ahead with its new-found way of raising tax money the argument Mason and other Americans used against the laws was not that rum or books would cost more *but that the British Constitution itself was violated by such taxes.*

Mason was no lawyer, but he was well-read in the law because his uncle, John Mercer, owned a teeming library. Mason also had an affinity for going to the heart of a matter, much as a good lawyer must do. To Mason and other Americans angered by the new taxes the British Constitution—"the Palladium of our Liberties"—guaranteed an Englishman that he could not be taxed unless his representatives had approved the revenue bill. This idea of the British Constitution (for it was a concept, not a written document) was more principle than fact—for there were thousands of Englishmen who could not vote and yet they paid their taxes dutifully. But the theory was sanctified by many convictions generated out of the Puritan Revolution of the 17th century, so that by Queen Anne's time the English theorists spoke of representation and taxation in the same breath.

Surely Mason knew of John Locke's works and took to heart the Englishman's assertion that all good governments guaranteed their citizens life, liberty, and property. Mason certainly must have read the famous essays of Thomas Gordon and John Trenchard, which were collected as *Cato's Letters* early in the eighteenth century and savored by generations of English-Americans. What did the British Constitution promise to Englishmen (on either side of the Atlantic, as Mason and other Americans saw it)? The blessings of liberty were the warp and woof of the British Constitution, "Cato" noted, "where the People have no Masters but the Laws, and Magistracy are formed by the People or their Deputies; and no Demands are made upon them, but what are made by the Law, and they know to a Penny what to pay before it is asked; where they that exact from them more than the Law allows, are punishable by Law; and where the Legislators are equally bound by their own Acts, equally involved in the Consequences." Mason had first-hand experience in making laws himself, for he had served in the House of Burgesses briefly and found the work tedious, while the absence from home and plantation made the sacrifice too great. Still, Mason knew that every Virginia taxpayer dug into his purse or pocket because someone who represented him had voted for the levy. Even when they grumbled, the Americans paid taxes which their colonial legislatures had levied because these demands were constitutional.

The Sugar Act and its later companion bills seemed to Mason and his fellow Virginians to be unlawful steps toward slavery. The slavery Mason made so much of on the one hand was human bondage, and he was ashamed of his part in the obnoxious slave system. But when Mason's generation spoke of slavery as a political fact, they meant something quite different from the black man's bondage which they witnessed every day. "Slavery is, to live at the mere Mercy of another;

and a Life of Slavery is, to those who can bear it, a continual State of Uncertainty and Wretchedness, often an Apprehension of Violence, often the lingering Dread of a violent Death." This view from "Cato" was acceptable to Americans, as well as the next point, "and thus, to many Men, the Love of Liberty is beyond the Love of Life."

The seedling of "give me liberty or give me death" was planted by English theorists and took root in Virginia. The constitutional crisis grew straight from the insistence of Parliament that American rights were subordinate to Parliamentary rights. Looking back, it is remarkable that the American Revolution took its theoretical basis from the English writers who flourished in the aftermath of the seventeenth-century Glorious Revolution that converted Great Britain from a semi-feudal power into a constitutional monarchy. Algernon Sidney, Thomas Gordon, John Trenchard, and John Locke had a powerful influence upon Mason and his contemporaries who were searching for arguments against the British ministry after 1764. As Mason saw matters, the battles waged in 1640 and 1688 were not unlike the struggle he and other Americans were drawn into by George III's artful, designing ministers. The baneful spirit that had swept Sidney to martyrdom seem to swirl still through the streets of London.

One thing has to remembered about the colonial resistance to Great Britain, and that is the whole protest movement was unlike anything that had ever been seen. Of course ancient Rome and Greece had contended with rebellious colonies, but protests were always considered treasonous and thus harshly suppressed. In the Americans had been left alone internally while her trade was completely off guard. Liberalizing forces in England during the seventeenth century had left their mark. The English press was freer than that of any other country, and since 1695 censorship was more of a threat than a fact. England's ruling class had adopted the mercantilist system as national policy, so that distant colonial markets were thought necessary to give the country an economic equilibrium. In the days of Robert Walpole, the first Whig prime minister, American had been left along internally while her trade was channeled through English and Scottish ports to the rest of the world. To be sure, laws were on the books that many Americans and most crown officials winked at, but Walpole's light touch and "salutary neglect" of a restrictive commercial policy helped give the colonies a prosperity unknown in earlier days. "This nation is a trading nation and the prosperity of the trade is what ought to be principally in the

8

eyes of every gentleman of the House," Walpole told the House of Commons in 1739. It would have been difficult to find an American who disagreed or who did not accept the satellite role of the thirteen colonies in that commercial orbit.

The happy situation of mother country and dutiful colonies did not deteriorate overnight; and as often happens, the very thing which should have made the bond stronger in fact weakened the imperial relationship. France, Britain's ancient enemy, lost her foothold on the North American continent as a result of the French and Indian War. With Canada in British hands, it was logical to expect the thirteen colonies would soon become at least fourteen, and the dreadful terror of the frontier war whoop would all but cease.

Mason had not fought in the war but his good friend and neighbor, George Washington, had been a prominent military leader in the first engagements and in the final capture of Fort Duquesne. The English victory had one particularly pleasing effect for Mason in that his investment in trans-Allegheny lands seemed secure with the French threat in the Ohio valley removed. With the war over, Mason and his neighbors the Lees looked forward to huge profits from the acres held by the Ohio Company and similar speculative ventures.

For several reasons, Mason and his Virginia partners in speculation had their smug expectations jarred. For one thing, the British were not eager to have the wild western country overrun with settlers who would ruin the profitable London fur trade. For another, Englishmen in high places held rival land claims, and they had powerful friends who could block the Virginians from gaining a final, free title to the western tracts. And finally, there was the problem—mentioned earlier—of the mounting national debt and the reaction of clever Englishmen to the clamor over heavy taxes from English landlords. The plan to shift some of this burden to the Americans came from George Grenville, Chancellor of the Exchequer, and when he made the proposal and explained the purpose as affording tax relief for home constituents the reaction in Parliament was a loud huzzah. Thus was born the Sugar Act, and so there began the long quarrel between the mother country and her colonies over the taxing power—a controversy that culminated in the Battle of Yorktown seventeen years later.

In the interval, however, the Americans tried to coax George III's ministers back to an observance of the old rules and the lax regulations of the 1750s. Insofar as George Mason and his Virginia neighbors were concerned, the year 1759 long stood out as one of the happiest in memory for the plain reason that tobacco prices then rose to an all-time high of forty shillings per hundredweight. No wonder that planters who rebelled in 1776 looked back on 1759 with nostalgia, for with good land producing one thousand pounds of tobacco per acre a large estate could clear profits of heady proportions. If a Virginian had to worry, he preferred to concentrate his anxiety on the price of land and tobacco—or even slaves—rather than on some distant Englishman's concern over a growing national debt. Indeed, the idea of a national debt was so vague most Virginians could hardly grasp the complexities of governmental finance involved; for in Virginia the income of the colony and its expenditures were in fairly nice balance. The private debts of some planters was another matter.

George Mason's own books were in good order, however, and he was inclined to look upon government finance as good businessmen often do: if they can run their affairs prudently, why can't the government do the same? Thus when George Grenville captivated the Tory politicians in England and seemed to be a financial genius, George Mason saw instead a cheap imitation of Pericles in the English minister. Lacking Pericles' "Genius or Abilitys," Mason said, Grenville and his minions had "dared to act the part that Pericles did, when He engaged his Country in the Peloponesian War; which, after a long & dreadful Scene of Blood, ended in the Ruin of all Greece." Clearly, Mason warned, Grenville's course would be equally disastrous to England.

Mason's view came as hindsight, after Englishmen had listened to Grenville and believed his program offered a way out of what seemed to be a morass of public debt. The solution seemed so simple, for what Grenville offered in 1765 was only a small tax on legal documents, newspapers, and playing cards. Englishmen had been paying the tax for years, and so it appeared harmless as a device to make colonials pay a bit of the burden. The English gentry were enthralled with the tax, for it offered them some relief, and as Grenville explained it there was no room for argument. Even wise Benjamin Franklin saw no great harm in the scheme, and recommended a good friend for the tax collector's job back in Philadelphia.

Nonetheless, the Stamp Act proved to be the beginning of the end for the old British-American relationship. Newspaper printers and those who wrote essays for their gazettes and journals, given time to prepare for the fateful day when the stamped paper would be required by law, used reams of paper to heap invective on the Britons who had concocted the taxing scheme. Carefully separating the ministry from the king, the pamphleteers and newspaper essayists flayed the English ministry as greedy taxgatherers bent on turning Americans into slaves. Public opinion—never before a matter of concern in British-American colonial affairs—was so violently aroused that George III's cabinet spent the next decade attempting to calm the Americans down.

They never could, and George Mason's reaction to the Stamp Act crisis typified the reason for the Englishmen's distress. As a vestryman of Truro Parish, he owed a dual allegiance to God and the king, but as a Virginian Mason also believed he had heavier responsibilities to his family and his country. Seated beside his pretty wife, Ann Eilbeck Mason, the master of Gunston Hall presided over a shiny mahogany dining board where six little faces looked up as their father finished saying grace.* We can safely assume that in the summer of 1765, George Mason finished his mealtime prayer with an additional remark or two about the return of the good old days—when Parliament knew its place, and kept it.

---

* The Masons had six surviving children by 1765. John, Elizabeth, and Thomas were born between 1766 and 1770.

Ann Eilbeck Mason, soon after her marriage to George Mason in 1750. After destroyed original by John Hesselius. *Courtesy of the Virginia Museum of Fine Arts and the Board of Regents of Gunston Hall.*

Chapter II

A Call to "A-ms"

ALONG with many other Americans who were aroused by the implications of the Stamp Act, Mason viewed the obnoxious bill as a personal problem. The law, which was scheduled to go into effect on November 1, 1765, obliged colonists to use stamped paper in their legal proceedings—but Virginians would have none of this nefarious stamped paper around. The dilemma posed was whether conducting legal business would be risky without stamped paper, and specifically, what would happen to evicted tenants who had not paid their rents? Mason obviously had discussed the matter with his neighbors from Belvoir and Mount Vernon, for late in December he drafted a plan that gave landlords a means of evading the Stamp Act.

As it happened, Parliament soon repealed the Stamp Act, so the plan never had to be used; but the anti-slavery preamble to the "scheme for replevying goods under distress for rent" sets the document apart from other protests against the Stamp Act. Indeed, Mason went out of his way to call attention to the growing evil Virginia planters condoned by their daily practices:

> The Policy of encouraging the Importation of free People & discouraging that of Slaves has never been duly considered in this Colony, or we shou'd not at this Day see one Half of our best Lands in most Parts of the Country remain unsetled, & the other cultivated with Slaves; not to mention the ill Effect such a Practice has upon the Morals & manners of our People: one of the first Signs of the Decay, & perhaps the primary Cause of the Destruction of the most flourishing Government that ever existed was the Introduction of great Numbers of Slaves—an Evil very pathetically described by the Roman Historians—but 'tis not the present Intention to expose our Weakness by examining this Subject too freely.

Mason could not resist the opportunity to deplore the effect of slavery, but he was also realist enough to know that the country was in no mood for an anti-slavery crusade. Whether anyone besides the Fairfaxes and Washingtons read Mason's indictment is uncertain, but undoubtedly the point hit a mark in the master of Mount Vernon, who shared Mason's abhorrence of human bondage and would in his will free his slaves.

For Mason, the Stamp Act troubles had a personal family tinge. His cousin, George Mercer, had been in London when the bill passed and had obtained an appointment as the Virginia distributor of stamped paper. The job seemed safe enough, and promised a steady income, but when Mercer's ship landed at Yorktown and the news reached Williamsburg, Mason's hapless kinsman was suddenly no welcomed hero but rather a turncoat villain. The act was due to go into force in a couple of days, and an angry crowd confronted Mercer on a Williamsburg street to demand his immediate resignation. Mercer was in danger of bodily harm when Governor Fauquier took him by the arm and led Mercer through the crowd. At the Governor's Palace the two talked it over and Fauquier finally asked Mercer "whether he was afraid for his Life ... if not his Honor and interest both demanded he should hold the office." Mercer resigned. Within hours Mercer was back on the ship, bound for London, and Mason never saw his ill-fated cousin again. Whatever regret Mason may have felt for Mercer as a relative was probably overborne in Mason's mind by the embarrassment of Mercer's attempt to find a soft job in such circumstances. Both men seemed to want to forget the whole thing as soon as possible.

After the Stamp Act troubles finally blew over, Mason was willing enough to go back to the halcyon days when Americans all along the seaboard considered England and the magnificent British navy as the best of protectors. When news of the repeal had first reached America in the spring of 1766, the reaction was one of rejoicing. "Illuminations & Sky-rockets proclaimed the general Joy," a sour-faced Loyalist, Peter Oliver, later recalled. "But it was not the Joy of Gratitude, but the Exultation of Triumph. *America* had now found a Way of redressing her own Grievances" while "thinking Minds compared the Proceedings of the parent State to the whirligig Toy wch. plays backward & forward for meer Amusement." Indeed, the British ministers were confused, and in their dilemma had finally taken their cue from the powerful British merchants who besieged

Parliament with letters and petitions asking that the Stamp Act be repealed so that they could get back to "business as usual."

There were several discordant notes, however, in the manner of repealing the despised act; and the more Mason thought about these outcroppings of British paternalism the less he liked them. A letter addressed to Americans from "a Committee of Merchants in London" had a particularly upsetting effect on Mason. The merchants urged Americans to be grateful for the repeal and their tone was patronizing. First, Mason thought, it was bad manners of the British to treat America with "the authoritative Style of a Master to a School-Boy." The English seemed to be saying to their upstart colonies "pray be a good boy for the future," Mason concluded, "do what your Papa and Mamma bid you, & hasten to return them your most grateful Acknowledgements for condescending to let you keep what is your own . . . but if you are a naughty Boy, & turn obstinate, & don't mind what your Papa & Mamma say to you . . . then every-body will hate you, & say you are a graceless & undutiful Child; [and] your Parents & Masters will be obliged to whip you severely. . . ."

Instead of chastisement, Mason thought, England owed it to the colonies to say that such a mistake as the Stamp Act would never again pass Parliament. However, the House of Commons had reacted in a surly manner, repealing the Stamp Act but at the same time passing the Declaratory Act (which said that the power of Parliament remained supreme "in all Cases whatsoever"). This kind of language, Mason said, was provocative—for the power of taking away a colonist's money (through taxes which he had no part in levying) was still left in Parliament. Unjust actions had preceded the Stamp Act—informers had been used by crown officials and efforts made "to drag a Freeman a thousand Miles from his own Country" and try him before a corrupt judge. So grievances still existed, Mason warned, and repeal of the Stamp Act had not calmed all the troubled Anglo-American waters.

Nevertheless, there was a great deal of huzzahing and toasting of George III when the Stamp Act was repealed. The Virginians joined with the neighbors in praising the English spirit of fair play and the British Constitution. The odious importation of slaves continued, and the Virginia House of Burgesses was in the same dilemma white men had continally faced—the taxes on slave imports helped support the expenses of government—so there was talk about the evils of slavery and some pious wishes that the demeaning system could be outlawed. But otherwise nobody did anything to stop the traffic in human beings.

The Americans' wish that the course of life could return to its pre-1758 channels was not to be. British ministers continually felt a strain on the national treasury, and in 1767 Charles Townshend, Chancellor of the Exchequer, urged Parliament to pursue a harder line with the colonies. As the English politician saw matters, the British army protected the American frontier while the British navy kept sea lanes open for American commerce. Why should Britons alone pay for the upkeep of an army, a navy, and the other growing expenses of government? Following this logic, Parliament listened to Townshend and voted for the taxes he proposed. Duties were placed on paper, glass, lead, painters' colors, and tea. The old duty on molasses was reduced, but crown officials were no longer supposed to wink at the law. Before 1763, British taxes levied in America totaled less than £2,000 a year, but after Townshend's plan went into operation the American consumers paid £30,000 a year. Customs regulations were tightened, smugglers were arrested in droves, and the machinery for enforcing tax collections was set in motion.

Most of the American protest that came in reaction to the Townshend duties was centered in the mercantile cities of Boston, New York, and Philadelphia where the taxes hit hardest. Newspapers and pamphlets were again full of denunciations of British policy, so that the memory of Stamp Act arrogance was revived. The customs officers were reviled as a set of thieves sent from England "to plunder our trade and drain the country of its money." At Charleston, the only large southern port, a leading merchant wailed that the customs officers were akin to the "miscreants who were driven out of the temple by Jesus with a scourge of small cords." Implicit in all the American reactions was a growing feeling that Parliament had again overstepped its bounds, and in Virginia as elsewhere the talk was of an economic reprisal. Merchants' committees had already met in the large cities, shaping up Non-Importation associations for subscribers who would promise to buy no English goods until the Townshend duties were repealed.

In Virginia, Mason and his neighbors in Fairfax County wanted to join in the protest, but without a large city where commerce centered there was no place where the resentment could crystalize until the Burgesses met in Williamsburg for their session. In these circumstances, various leaders circulated plans drawn by Philadelphians for their own inspection and use. One such plan came to Washington's hand, and he apparently passed it around Truro Parish. At the election Washington had been chosen again to represent Fairfax County, and he seems to have called on his neighbors for their opinion as to what action Virginia ought to take when the House of Burgesses met in May. Out of some informal conferences and exchanges by post riders the Virginia Non-Importation Association of 1769 took shape.

Mason carefully examined the Philadelphia merchants' plan which Washington had sent him. In his covering letter, the master of Mount Vernon had suggested that paper protests were becoming tiresome. "It seems highly necessary that some thing shou'd be done to avert the stroke and maintain the liberty which we have derived from our Ancestors; but the manner of doing it to answer the purpose effectually is the point in question," Washington wrote. "That no man shou'd scruple, or hesitate a moment to use A-ms in defence of so valuable a blessing, on which all the good and evil of life depends; is clearly my opinion; yet A-ms I wou'd beg leave to add, should be the last resource; the denier [sic] resort." Washington could not bring himself to say that militant protests might be needed to reinforce paper ones, so he did not write the missing "r" in "A-ms." But clearly Mason knew what Washington meant, and yet in 1769 the ultimate use of the weapons of war to bring about a change in British policy seemed remote.

Although he had been thinking along the same lines, Mason was suffering from "a Disorder which affects my Head & Eyes in such a Manner that I am totally incapable of Business." Therefore, he deferred to the ideas others had on the subject of non-importation, promising to turn his attention to the economic sanctions when he felt better. Meanwhile, a local plan based on the Philadelphia merchants' plea came to Washington's hand, and he again dispatched this plan to Mason. Mason made some suggested changes, which Washington accepted, and this plan was placed in the Fairfax burgess' saddle bags. Along with a pledge that Virginians buy no articles taxed under Townshend's bill, the Non-Importation Associators were also pledged not to import any slaves "until the said Acts of Parliament are repeal'd." A hint of further economic barriers was added, even to the stoppage of the all-important tobacco trade, if Parliament did not repeal the loathed duties.

By the time Washington reached Williamsburg (after nursing a sick horse along the so-called "burgesses' route from Fredericksburg) there was much talk concerning the proper steps to air colonial grievances. The newly-arrived royal governor, Lord Botetourt, was a pleasant man who disliked scenes, and to tell the truth, there were many Virginians who thought there was no reason to become violent over a threepenny tax on tea. Mason's friends, Arthur and Richard Henry Lee, were in the group that favored extreme measures and their writings reflected the thinking of the northern Neck gentry who would lead the colony down the road to revolution. Arthur Lee's "Monitor" letters in the *Virginia Gazette* showed a determination to resist Parliament at every turn, and Mason himself may have been the author of the "Atticus" letters printed in the Williamsburg newspaper during May 1769. In the crisis which Britain had fomented, "Atticus" charged, an "unaccountable System of Politics, has been adopted, and we are not allowed to purchase the Manufactures of our Mother-Country, unless loaded with Taxes to raise a Revenue from us, without our Consent." A refusal to buy British goods and an embargo on American exports to England, "Atticus" reasoned, ought to bring the English to their senses. "These are the Arms with which GOD and Nature have furnished us for our Defence." And there it was—the vaguest hint—that arms might be used to accomplish a fairer plan, but only if the paper weapons and personal conduct failed to bring Parliament around to the American viewpoint. The conclusion of the second "Atticus" letter was surely Mason's idea. Impose economic sanctions on the English and they would be forced to understand what the ministers had unwittingly done to British-American relations. "Their own Interest wou'd quickly awaken their Attention: They would see, They wou'd feel the Oppressions we groan under, and exert themselves effectually on our Behalf: A candid and thorough Examination wou'd be brought on, and the Conduct of the Ministry exposed in its proper Light." Notice where the burden of blame fell—on the British ministers who had concocted the taxing scheme. They were the villains in the drama, and Parliament was clearly called upon to turn these rascals out.

Conversations, newspaper essays, and personal letters did their work. On May 16 the House of Burgesses passed resolutions calling for the "sole Right of imposing Taxes on the Inhabitants of . . . Virginia." Other resolves affirmed the right of citizens to petition their legislature and protested the transporting of accused Americans to England for trial. Lord Botetourt at once ordered the session ended (as was his right) on the ground that the Burgesses had exceeded their authority. But the whole business that followed was conducted with fitting dignity, for these revolutionaries did not storm the palace gates or throw stones through Lord Botetourt's windows. Instead they withdrew to the Raleigh Tavern, set themselves up as an *ad hoc* protest committee, and used the plan Washington had brought down from Fairfax County as their outline. On May 18, eight-eight burgesses signed the Virginia Non-Importation Agreement, drank appropriate toasts to "The King" and "The Constitutional British Liberty in America"; and then those who were invited "went to the Queen's Birth Night at the Palace." In that short entry in his diary Washington told how the radicals of 1769 chose to go about their business. They decided on a course of action and then accepted the governor's invitation to celebrate the Queen's birthday at his palace ball, without the slightest feeling of inconsistency.

Could these be the men who would someday drill on the common at Bowling Green, or at Orange Court House, or on the greensward by the Williamsburg powder magazine? Years would have to pass before the thrill of being a British subject gave away to the sense of righteousness which is always part of a rebel. It took Mason, Washington, and the other leading Virginians more days and distresses than they cared to recall before they finally concluded that Parliament would not listen to their pleas. The economic boycott had some effect on England, and the crisis passed in part because months went by and not much happened.

Then, something took place in Boston and as a result, Virginia was never the same again.

Chapter III

The Firebrand from Fairfax County

FROM the distance of almost two centuries it often seems that the American colonies from the Stamp Act onward were thirteen localities of seething unrest. In truth, life went on in the colonies before and after 1765 with a steadiness unrelated to political concerns, particularly in areas where there were no towns—and that meant most of Virginia. For the protests of the 1760s were generated in the port cities of British North America and only spread to the countryside after the Boston Port Bill.

When Parliament began to turn the screws on colonial Americans, with threats of bayonets and bagpiping regiments, this upset the town residents who saw the redcoats in their streets. Since most colonial Americans lived in the country, however, the friction between the colonies and England was something they heard about at market days or read about in the newspapers, but hardly experienced personally. Farmers were involved in the non-importation boycotts only indirectly, for not many of them were larger buyers of such forbidden articles as "Silks of all Sorts, except Sewing Silk, Cambrick, Lawn, Muslin, Gauze, except Boulting Cloths, Callico or Cotton Stuffs of more than Two Shillings per Yard, Linen" and other goods which the farmer's wives coveted but could not afford. Homespun linsey-woolsey was the fabric on most American backs, and the fine wines boycotted by the non-importation agreements never graced their tables anyway.

George Mason knew this, of course, but he and the other Virginia protestors of parliamentary power realized that England was mighty but vulnerable. England had become a trading nation, with commerce on an international scale vital to her well-being. This was the end result of mercantilist policies and any breakdown of foreign or colonial markets would give pause to the ruling party, the Americans reasoned. Thus the after-dinner hours at Gunston Hall, when Washington, Richard Henry Lee, Bryan Fairfax, and other thoughtful men were enjoying Mason's hospitality, must have been full of earnest discussions on ways and means for bringing pressure on English merchants. As Edmund S. Morgan has shown, the Stamp Act was repealed more because of the protests of the suffering English merchants than in response to the American pleas for colonial rights. Mason must have realized this fact, and his sense of disappointment when the non-importation boycotts began to falter was certain. The way to enforce the boycott, Mason reasoned, was to expose the violators to public scorn. Men had pledged their word that they would not buy goods on the enumerated list of imported English articles, then by stealth had broken their promise. "I don't see how these Regulations can be effected by any other Means than appointing Committees in the Countys," Mason observed, "to examine from Time to Time into the Imports, & to convey an Account of any Violation of the Association to the Moderator, to be by him publish'd, or by a Committee appointed for that purpose in Wmsburg." What upset Mason was that "the Custom-House Books shew'd that the Exports to Virginia in particular were very little, if at all, lessened" by the boycott. The plain truth was that in spite of the signatures on non-importation agreements, Virginians were importing more goods in 1770 than they had in 1769, by an increase of £229,420.

The embarrassment was severe and the remedy—committees of inspection called "Associators"—were established in some counties. They proved, in general, ineffective. The price of tobacco, wheat, and lumber, was high enough that farmers, mill and plantation owners were doing well; and as the protestors found, it is difficult to arouse the general public during times of economic prosperity. The Boston Massacre in 1770 excited New England and caused ripples to the southward, but Mason was like most of the colonists in his wait-and-see attitude. Late in 1770 he wrote a relative in England that the boycott had all but failed, although a reconciliation with the mother country would erase all the animosity. "But shou'd the oppressive System of taxing us without our Consent be continued," he warned, "The Flame, however smother'd now, will break out the redoubled Ardour, & the Spirit of Opposition (Self-defence is its' proper Name) wear a more formidable Shape than ever—more formidable, because more natural & practicable."

Mason was inclined to blame the collapse of the economic resistance to the hurried way the ban on English imports had been thrown up, and to the disposition of many Americans to purchase goods they did not need. *"Luxury & Ostentation"* had produced weaknesses in the plan, Mason said, but happily the whole scheme could be forgotten if England would only grant Americans their exclusive right to tax themselves. "We know that our Happiness our very Being depends upon our Connection with our Mother Country," Mason admitted. "But we will not submit to have our own Money taken out [of] our Pockets without our Consent. . . . We owe to our Mother-Country the Duty of Subjects but will not pay her the Submission of Slaves." No colonial essayist stated the argument more neatly. As Mason saw the matter he was really only arguing that Englishmen ought to see that in granting the American demands they were only preserving "the Vigour & Spirit of her own free happy Constitution."

Men's perceptions on both sides of the Atlantic differed greatly, however. The more Parliament debated the taxing problem, the more the British ministry became convinced that many Americans aimed only at total independence. A Loyalist historian, Peter Oliver, later claimed that although the colonies declared themselves independent in 1776, the issue "was settled in *Boston,* in 1768, by *Adams* & his Junto." Thus from a New England vantage point it appeared that Samuel Adams and his friends in the Caucus Club and Loyal Nine had been the generators of independence. From below the Potomac there were stirrings before 1768, however, and by the summer of 1771 (when most of the colonies were content to give up the boycott on all English imports except tea) Mason and the committee of associators in Fairfax County continued their vigilance and denounced those merchants who had scuttled the patriots' efforts around Alexandria. Washington and Mason wrote Peyton Randolph, the moderator of the Virginia Non-importation Association, an appeal for vigilance so that well-intentioned merchants who observed the ban would not "find themselves . . . greatly embarrassed in their business, and their trade daily falling into the hands of men, who have not acted upon the same honourable principles."

Months passed, and the colonists kept up a token protest by not buying as much tea from English exporters, but 1771 and 1772 were relatively calm years. Mason turned his attention to Ohio Company affairs and continued to buy headrights for lands. At Gunston Hall his wife presented him with two more sons, and another daughter.

But in March 1773 tragedy interrupted the pleasant flow of life at the plantation; Ann Mason, in her thirty-ninth year and possessed of the full "Beauty of her Person, & the Sweetness of her Disposition," died shortly after a long, "painful & tedious illness." The blow fell on Mason as he was at the pinnacle of personal success, for he owned over five thousand acres in the vicinity of Gunston Hall, a good stock of cash, over a hundred slaves, and shares in thousands of western acres. Mason's friend, the Reverend James Scott, came to give the funeral sermon at Pohick Church.

> "Whom have I in heaven but thee? and there is none upon earth
> that I desire beside thee—"

The minister read from the 73rd Psalm. Ann Mason's body was brought to the family cemetery at Gunston Hall, and then for many months Mason grieved for his young wife.

To occupy his mind with other matters, Mason had the care of his nine children and a fearsome amount of detail shoved his way by the Ohio Company business. Black nursemaids helped with the children, and Mason's small but well-chosen library aided in the other chore. He read the charters of Virginia and her neighbors, pored over law books for interpretations of land laws, and sharpened his knowledge of the history of Virginia from the days at Jamestown. Slowly Mason regained his composure and found that in supervising the planting of trees, in buying a tract there and selling another there, and in riding around Gunston Hall's several farms the pace of life was still the same although his thoughts and steps often turned to Ann Mason's grave.

As luck would have it, Mason returned to the everyday world of business at about the time the business world was about to go—in America—on a cockeyed course. Eager to protect his land interests, Mason had traveled to Williamsburg in May 1774 to obtain concessions while the General Assembly was in session. To his neighbor, Martin Cockburn, Mason described the Williamsburg scene.

Williamsburg, May 26th, 1774.
Dear Sir
I arrived here on Sunday morning last, but found every body's attention so entirely engrossed by the Boston affair, that I have as yet done nothing respecting my charter-rights and, I am afraid, shall not this week.
A dissolution of the House of Burgesses is generally expected;

but I think will not happen before the House has gone though the public business, which will be late in June.

Whatever resolves or measures are intended for the perservations of our rights and liberties, will be reserved for the conclusion of the session. Matters of that sort here are conducted and prepared with a great deal of privacy, and by very few members; of whom Patrick Henry is the principal.

At the request of the gentlemen concerned, I have spent an evening with them upon the subject, where I had an opportunity of conversing with Mr. Henry, and knowing his sentiments; as well as hearing him speak in the house since, on different occasions. He is by far the most powerful speaker I ever heard. Every word he says not only engages but commands the attention; and your passions are no longer your own when he addresses them. But his eloquence is the smallest part of his merit. He is in my opinion the first man upon this continent, as well in abilities as public virtures, and had he lived in Rome about the time of the first Punic war, when the Roman people had arrived at their meridian glory, and their virture not tarnished, Mr. Henry's talents must have put him at the head of that glorious Commonwealth.

Inclosed you have the Boston Trade Act, and a resolve of our House of Burgesses. You will observe it is confined to the members of their own House: but they would wish to see the example followed through the country; for which purpose the members at their own private expense, are sending expresses with the resolve to their respective counties. Mr. Massey will receive a copy of the resolve from Col. Washington; and should a day of prayer and fasting be appointed in our county, please to tell my dear little family that I charge them to pay strict attention to it, and that I desire my three eldest sons, and my two eldest daughters, may attend church in mourning, if they have it, as I believe they have.

I begin to grow heartily tired of this town and hope to be able to leave it some time next week, but of this, I can't yet be certain. I beg to be tenderly remembered to my children, and am, with my compliments to my cousins and yourself, Dear Sir, Your affectionate and obedient servant,

G Mason.

Thus by coincidence was Mason in Williamsburg when movement against British policy shifted from strongly-worded protests to outrage. The tar-and-feathers remedy practiced in New England had not spread to Virginia, but the Boston Port Bill created a common cause. Henceforth, the colonies stood together and there would be only one of two solutions—a backing down by the British or the colonists. If neither retreated, the consequences had to result in civil war.

Patrick Henry impressed Mason so strongly that for the next fourteen years the two men were usually in unison on their political principles. Their closeness is all the more remarkable in that Jefferson particularly, and Madison and Washington so some degree—came to distrust Henry as a demagogue. Mason was the only Virginia patriot who moved back and forth from Henry to Jefferson or Madison and still retained the confidence of all.

The "resolve of the House of Burgesses" which Mason mentioned had set June 1 as the "Day of Fasting, Humiliation, and Prayer" to express sympathy with the closing of Boston harbor on that same day. Mason saw the punitive Boston Port Bill in the May 19 *Virginia Gazette* and he soon hurried back to Gunston Hall to observe the ritual of protest at Pohick Church.

Within a week he probably had also written his own special form of anti-British propaganda, for the Prince William County Resolves of June 6 (passed at the Dumfries courthouse meeting) bear the stylistic verve of Mason's prose. "No person ought to be taxed but by his own consent," the Resolves began, "expressed either by himself or his Representatives. . . . Resolved, That the city of Boston, in the Massachusetts Bay, is now suffering in the common cause of American liberty, and on account of its opposition to an Act of the British Legislature, for imposing a duty upon tea, to be collected in *America*." The resolutions then called upon the counties to take such proper and salutary measures as will essentially conduce to a repeal of those Acts of Parliament which had brought on the crisis. The House of Burgesses had been prorogued, and the means of acting in unison was left to county committees of correspondence.

Fortunately for the patriots, the crisis came in the spring when the roads were passable and the winds fair. Soon other counties joined with resolutions calling for stout resistance to British measures. Mason and Washington talked the situation over, and it seemed that one prediction in *Cato's Letters* (number 67) was coming to fulfillment. Foreseeing the time when colonies would strain at the leash, the essayist had in 1722 predicted that the American colonies would "by the natural course of human Affairs . . . at last grow too powerful and unruly to be governed by our [British] interest only." Indeed, that time had come. Early in July Fairfax County patriots pledged £273 in cash, 38 barrels of flour, and 150 bushels of wheat as relief for their comrades in Boston. On Sunday, July 17, Mason rode to Mount Vernon and consulted Washington on the proper steps for the county committee of safety, which had become the de facto governing body. That night Mason must have been busy at the writing desk, for by that next morning he had jotted down the results of his talks with Washington—the Fairfax County Resolves of 1774—a document considered by some historians as the signal torch of the American Revolution.

The defiant tone of the Fairfax Resolves was meant to set the record straight. Virginians were not conquered men but the descendants "of the Conquerors," and therefore all the rights of Englishmen were part of their heritage including the most valuable principle of all: ". . . the People's being governed by no Laws, to which they have not given their Consent, by Representatives freely chosen by themselves." Since Americans were not represented in Parliament, the only legislatures they were bound to follow were those of each colony; and attempts by Parliament to tax the colonists were "diametrically contrary to the first principles of the [British] Constitution." The claims of Parliament to supreme power over the colonies were denounced as productive of "the most grievous and intollerable Species of Tyranny and Oppression, that ever was inflicted upon Mankind." Strong language from angry men, and there was more to come. There were twenty-four resolutions in all, with further calls for bans on imports (particularly on slaves and any items tending to encourage "all Manner of Luxury and Extravagance"), a stoppage of lumber exports to the West Indies, and a continuance of the non-importation associations. Persons who violated the boycott were to be publicly listed so that "such Traitors to their Country may be publickly known and detested." A petition to George III was urged, to come from a Continental Congress, "asserting with decent Firmness our just and constitutional Rights." Finally, Washington and Charles Broadwater were appointed to the convention called to meet in Williamsburg on August 1 to consider "the Measures proper to be taken in the present alarming and dangerous Situation of America."

In writing the Fairfax County Resolves, Mason had assumed that the British ministry was recklessly in pursuit of "a premeditated Design and System . . . to introduce an arbitrary Government into his Majesty's American Dominions; to which End they are artfully prejudicing our Sovereign, and inflaming the Minds of our fellow-Subjects in Great Britain." This conspiracy theory was widely held in America during the 1770s and was used to rationalize the American homage to the King while his ministers seemed to be placing their boots on American necks.

As Mason and other Americans saw matters, George III was misinformed and misled by designing ministers. Once the truth came home to the Court of St. James, as a petition from Congress would prove, the king would set the whole crisis aside by his magnanimous and just policies. It took some doing, but that theory finally fell with a loud thump in the winter of 1775-1776, and Mason was one of the first to see that the pretense of George III as the all-wise, loving monarchy was without justification.

For the moment, however, there was much to be done. The Fairfax committee set about to see that the boycott on British imports was clamped down with vigor. More food and money was collected to help the beleaguered Bostonians. The county militia was urged to place its officers and men in a state of readiness, with muskets and rifles kept in good repair and sufficient powder stored in case of an emergency. To keep the appearance of dutiful subjects, the bustle for militia weapons and powder was, ostensibly, owing to anticipated frontier skirmishes with Indians. The Fairfax Militia Association, with Colonel Mason presiding, met on September 21 to discuss their next steps, for Parliament had said that unless the tea destroyed in Boston harbor was paid for, the Boston harbor would have a blockade of indefinite duration.

"In this Time of Extreme Danger," Colonel Mason charged, "with the Indian Enemy in our Country, and threat'ned with the Destruction of our Civil-rights, & Liberty, and all that is dear to British Subjects & Freemen," every militia member had a solemn duty to perform. They would form "The Fairfax independent Company of Voluntiers" and elect officers, practice "the military Exercise & Discipline" and wear blue uniforms with buff-colored piping and lapels. Each coat would have "plain yellow metal Buttons," and every soldier and officer would be "furnished with a good Fire-lock & Bayonet, Sling Cartouch-Box, and Tomahawk" at his own expense. "We will, each of us, constantly keep by us a Stock of six pounds of Gunpowder, twenty pounds of Lead, and fifty Gun-flints, at the least."

What Mason and the coopers and millers in the Fairfax Independent Company also knew was that Colonel George Washington would give them the benefit of his experience. And Colonel Washington, clad in his blue-and-buff uniform, was no mean figure. For his part, Mason would see that they had lead and flints from Maryland or the Continental Congress, and more if needed. The next move was up to Lord North and his supporters.

Parliament showed the colonists that there was to be no backing down on their part. The Intolerable Acts, as the Americans came to call them, seemed a dangling threat over other colonies as the charter of Massachusetts was suspended and troops quartered in places commandeered from the local citizens. In Massachusetts town meetings were not to be held without the royal governor's approval, while the sheriff was to be appointed by this royal official who would in turn pick juries. All that was bad enough for what appeared to be the punishment in store for any over-zealous colony, but what concerned Mason and many Virginians in particular was the Quebec Act of 1774, which extended jurisdiction over part of the Ohio Valley to the province of Quebec and jeopardized land titles west of an arbitrary Indian boundary line. Thousands of pounds and more hours might be wasted if the British decree stood unchallenged, for conflicting land claims in an arbitrarily extended Quebec were the last thing Virginia land speculators wanted.

While the pace of protest quickened, Mason kept busy by dividing his time between the business of Gunston Hall and the preparations at Alexandria. Mason's oldest son, who had inherited some of his father's disabilities, was elected a militia ensign and given some small tasks for the committee of safety. In the conversations after church on Sunday and around the crossroads taverns it is likely that the condition of every militiaman's musket and the owner's accuracy was discussed, and some informal target practice was soon under way. When the first Continental Congress was held in Philadelphia in September 1774, Mason's acquaintance Peyton Randolph—a dignified and likeable man of large proportions—was chosen as its president. Patrick Henry and Richard Henry Lee, the two Virginians whom Mason admired most, were also on the delegation. Their radical stance had Mason's full support, and the Declaration of Rights approved by the Congress in October 1774 was a document full of appeal to the master of Gunston Hall. The plea of Parliament for a return to the situation of 1763, and a recognition that the colonies alone could raise taxes, was bound to provoke an angry rejoinder from Parliament. However, the men at Philadelphia who passed the Declaration believed that it was they who were the true defenders of the British Constitution.

So did Mason. When Mason looked back on the scenes of 1775-1776 a short time later, he insisted that even as late as the battle of Lexington-Concord he was still hopeful of a reconciliation with England. "No man was more warmly attach'd to the Hanover Family & the Whig Interest of England than I was, & few Men had stronger Prejudices in Favour of that Form of Government under which I was born & bred, or a greater Aversion to changing it." What caused Mason to abandon hope? "As long as we had any well founded hopes of Reconciliation, I opposed, to the utmost of my Power, all violent Measures, & such as might shut the Door to it; but when Reconciliation became a lost Hope, when unconditional Submission, or effectual Resistance, were the only Alternatives left us, when the last dutiful & humble petition from Congress received no other Answer than declaring us Rebels . . . I from that Moment look'd forward to a Revolution & Independence."

That last hope, the so-called "Olive Branch Petition" to George III, was still six months away when Mason had helped place Fairfax County on a virtual wartime footing by ordering the collection of a three-shilling poll tax to buy arms and ammunition. Perhaps Mason and his friends really did believe there was still room for the possibility of a last-minute compromise, but they acted otherwise when they agreed to invite Maryland militiamen to cooperate with them to patrol the Potomac, and to raise a force composed of all able-bodied white males between the ages of sixteen and fifty. The door to conciliation was left open, only slightly ajar, by their call for action. The militant activities would "relieve our mother country from any expense in our protection and defence, [and] will obviate the pretence of a necessity for taxing us on that account, and render it unnecessary to keep Standing Armies among us." Sarcasm, of course, but also there was an ironic grain of truth in the committee of safety statement: if the troubles died way, then in the future Parliament would not need to tax Americans to keep troops stationed in the key ports.

Fortunately, Alexandria was too small a port to require a royal garrison or Virginians would have been more anxious than they were. As matters stood, the hue-and-cry was all in Boston, New York, and Philadelphia, where liberty poles were being cut down by redcoats one day and replaced by Sons of Liberty the next—or when mobs would form to harass the "lobster backs." Virginians read of these affrays in letters and newspapers, but the actual disturbances were hundreds of miles away. Preparedness seemed the order of the day. Early in February 1775 Mason took his plan "for Embodying the People"—we would call it mobilization in the 1970's—and laid out a course for Fairfax County citizens to follow:

> Threatened with the Destruction of our antient Laws & Liberty, and the Loss of all that is dear to British Subjects & Freemen, justly alarmed with the Prospect of impending Ruin, firmly determined, at the hazard of our Lives, to transmit to our Children & Posterity those Sacred Rights to which [we] ourselves were born; and thoroughly convinced that a well regulated Militia . . . is the natural Strength and only safe & stable security of a free Government . . . WE the Subscribers, Inhabitants of Fairfax County, have freely & voluntarily agreed , hereby do agree & solemnly promise, to enroll & embody ourselves into a Militia for this County. . . .

Perhaps at this juncture in history Mason and Washington thought that somehow they could turn back. Surely they were honorable men, not hypocrites (as the Tories later claimed) who went through motions but had no intention of ever toasting George III again. Notice, in this final call before the outbreak of fighting to the northward, that Mason concluded his plan with a justification for what had taken place and what was about to happen. The Fairfax County militia promised "that we will always hold ourselves in Readiness, in Case of Necessity, Hostile Invasion, or real Danger, to defend & preserve to the utmost of our Power, our Religion, the Laws of our Country, & the just Rights, & Privileges of our fellow Subjects, our Posterity, & ourselves, upon the Principles & Privileges of the English Constitution."

The hour was late—the blood-soaked earth of Lexington-Concord was three months away—yet Mason felt compelled to make one final appeal to the rights of Englishmen living under the venerated Constitution.

Gunston Hall. Opened to the public in 1952, Gunston Hall is owned by the Commonwealth of Virginia and administered by a Board of Regents appointed from the Colonial Dames of America. *Courtesy of the Board of Regents of Gunston Hall.*

Part of the restored gardens on the Potomac side of Gunston Hall. *Courtesy of the Board of Regents of Gunston Hall.*

Chapter IV

In Committees There Is Safety

"IN the Spring of 1775," a noted Boston Loyalist, Peter Oliver, recalled, "the War began to redden." Indeed, the redstained grass around the bridge at Concord was a signal to all the world, but the implications of the day-long battle did not seep into the colonists' consciousness as fast as the spilled blood soaked into the ridge above the famous bridge. For a decade there had been so much rhetoric that the din of charges and countercharges had almost become normal. Bad as conditions were, the number of Americans who thought a final military showdown necessary was few. In his heart of hearts, Mason did not expect that the strain of ten years would produce this terrible result. Yet when the open breach came, Mason had no hesitation—he pledged his life and his sacred honor to the cause of American freedom. If there was a noose waiting in London for George Washington's neck, there was another reserved for George Mason.

Such an unpleasant prospect was hardly ever alluded to, but Washington mentioned at least once the possibility of an English gallows for his last walk, and surely Mason knew the price that had to be paid in an English court for treason. But, who were the traitors? As Mason and the other American revolutionaries viewed the matter, *they* were the upholders of English liberties while the British ministers had been in a conspiracy to deny Anglo-Americans their rights. All the logic seemed to justify their actions in Williamsburg, Alexandria, Philadelphia, Boston, Providence, Charleston, or wherever the British flag was hauled down in the third week of April 1775. The war that finally began on April 19 was commonly shared news from the Maine district to Georgia by early May. Before George Washington's name became a household word in every colony, only the most naive America still hoped that somehow the atrocities of that fateful day could be forgotten in a general settlement of all the grievances building since 1765.

Only two days before Captain Parker's men waited near the bridge at Concord, the Fairfax County Committee of Safety reported on the progress of its assessments for weapons. On April 17 Mason gave Colonel Washington £31..17..0 in Virginia currency from the poll tax that had been collected to buy arms, and it was well to have matters settled because Washington was soon headed for Philadelphia and a higher destiny. Within the next ten days Mason considered the problem of defense in a new light, for apparently there had been a few squabbles about rank in the Fairfax Independent Company and Mason was disturbed.

"This part of the country has the glory of setting so laudable an example," Mason cautioned, "let us not tarnish it by any little dirty views of party, of mean self-interest or of low ambition." The best guide to the conduct of free men was to return to the people a fixed intervals "for their approbation or dissent. Whenever this is neglected or evaded, or the free voice of the people is suppressed or corrupted; or whenever any military establishment or authority is not, by some certain mode of rotation, dissolved into and blended with that mass from which it was taken, inevitable destruction to the state follows."

In short, Colonel Mason was saying, the best way to keep a society happy and free is to see that no one holds on to places of power too long. That historical example seemed confirmed by experience in ancient Rome, in "our mother county," England, and could happen in America, too. Instead of such corrupting influences, Mason proposed that offices in the militia be limited to a year's duration. "The proposed interval of a year will defeat undue influence or cabals; and the capacity of being rechosen afterwards, opens a door to the return of officers of approved merit, and will always be a means of excluding unworthy men, whom an absolute rotation would of necessity introduce." This seminal idea was firmly planted in Mason's mind, and he would remember it until his last days. Men in office are trustworthy, he seemed to say, only when they are constantly answerable to the citizens who elected them. There were exceptions to all such rules, of course, and his neighbor was one. Washington had been elected commander "by the unanimous voice of the company . . . [and] his choice is a very proper one, justly due to his public merit and experience." The selection of Washington was easily

The drawing room at Gunston Hall is a model of harmony and elegance.
Courtesy of the Board of Regents of Gunston Hall.

justified because "It is peculiarly suited to our circumstances, and was dictated, not by compliment, but conviction." On the other hand, gentlemen of Washington's abilities were scarce. Annual elections would guard against the tenure of the incompetent, the bully, or the braggart.

As it turned out, Washington only held his commission as the Fairfax militia colonel briefly. At Philadelphia he was selected to command the gathering army outside Boston, and he hastily wrote the Fairfax County Committee a letter of resignation. It was understood that Washington was leaving behind any responsibility to the county militia as he prepared to take over the command of nearly 14,000 men around Boston. Mason and other committeemen wished Washington Godspeed. For the moment, the British were bottled up on the Boston peninsula and there seemed no need to be overly concerned about what Governor Dunmore had done to the colony's powder stored at Williamsburg on April 21. Patrick Henry and his friends had moved with all haste to demand return of the powder, and Dunmore had skedaddled to the protection of a royal man o'war. In Fairfax County, however, things were quiet.

In fact, the situation was so calm in the Northern Neck that Mason and other planters began to assess the situation and decided that this was a now-or-never-moment to make money. They may sound crass or unpatriotic, but in the eighteenth century (as Locke had said on several occasions) the man of parts looked to life, and liberty, and property. If the war continued, a shortage of raw materials was an inevitable as was a royal naval blockade. So Mason and many other planters figured they had better ship their tobacco hogsheads to London while it was still possible.

Down to the loading docks Mason hustled, with one hundred wooden hogsheads crammed with choice Virginia oronoko tobacco which he calculated was worth £11 per hogshead, or £1,100 in all—a tidy sum that might be even larger if it reached the London auction market at the right time. Mason even sent the tobacco to Richard Henry Lee's brother, William, who was a consignment agent in London. His hopes for enormous profit went aglimmering however, for too many others had the same idea, and prices stayed low; and years later he was still hounding Lee for full payment of this last-minute effort to make a profit before all connection between England the America was broken asunder. There was much of the philosopher in Mason, to be sure, and we can guess that he somehow realized that he was a bit too eager to profit from a bad situation.

Other Americans were equally happy to find the war was creating a profitable situation for certain kinds of commerce, until the British naval blockade played havoc with colonial ships. Mason's small effort to realize a profit was nothing compared to the deals made by such merchant princes as Robert Morris and William Bingham of Philadelphia. By the end of 1775 Mason could see that the British market for American tobacco was gone and he accomodated himself to the realities, but others of a sharper mentality saw opportunities in the scarcities that war created. By the summer of 1776 Mason was in a different position, for as a legislator he was duty-bound to hold down prices and to place the country's interest above his own. But as certain items became scarce and venturesome shippers evaded the block-ading British, the lure of high profits overbore patriotic instincts. A business associate of Robert Morris's complained from Baltimore that Virginians were trying to discourage blockade-runners who brought in consumer goods instead of needed munitions. "Goods are dayly arriveing And the Virginians are determined to throw Every Obstacle in the way of Speculation," David Stewart of Baltimore complained.

Once Mason had dispatched his cargo to London, he joined the rest of the Committee of Safety in tending to the main business of defense. He was dismayed that Quaker merchants refused, on conscientious grounds, to pay their assessment for buying weapons. Then his neighbors embarrassed Mason by indicating that he was their choice to take Washington's place on the Fairfax delegation to the Virginia Convention of July 1775. Mason begged the freeholders not to elect him. "Reflect on the duty I owe to a poor little helpless family of orphans to whom I now must act the part of father and mother both, and how incompatible such an office would be with the daily attention they require," he wrote.

The excuse seemed plausible to Mason, but not to his peers, and they sent him off to Richmond for the extra-legal meeting. Mason reached Richmond by July 17 and a week later was reporting to a friend with tales of hard work, long hours, and the ever-present problem of money-raising. There was also a rumor that Mason's name would be thrown in nomination for Washington's vacant place in the Continental Congress. Mason expected George Wythe would take the general's seat, but "there will be other vacancies, [and] I have been a good deal pressed by some of my friends to serve at the Congress, but shall firmly persist in a refusal, and thereby I hope to prevent their making any such proposal in the Convention." Plainly, Mason had no taste for travel, and the dusty road to Richmond was about all he could stand.

Let others go to the capital of Pennsylvania, with its lighted and paved streets, high-ceilinged churches, and famous hostelries. At this moment, there was still hope of reconcilliation with England, and the last fateful petition to George III was in prospect. Mason was now fifty and thought of himself as an old man—the average man in the colonies then lived to be around thirty-five—and getting in and out of a saddle was a bit harder each year. His gouty feet ached, and his digestion was none too good. These bodily ills plus the nine mouths to feed at Gunston Hall gave Mason pause—and then caused him to beg off from any duty at Philadelphia. "I was publickly called upon . . . & obliged to make a public Excuse . . . in doing which I felt myself more distress'd than ever I was in my Life," he confessed. So far as we know, Mason never regretted his decision, even though it meant that he missed the chance to serve alongside his friend, Thomas Jefferson, on that great July day in history almost a year later.

Although Mason had tried to avoid service in the July 1775 Virginia convention, once he began working as a delegate in the muggy summer weather he found a lot of work somehow fell to him. For one thing, Mason was an impatient man who often preferred to do things alone and quickly than to await a long, drawn-out committee action. For another, Mason was inclined to take risks and hope that the whole situation would somehow work out. The Convention faced the £150,000 debt incurred by Lord Dunmore's War and still took on more. "Our Share of the Expence of the continental Army [is] £150,000 more, the Charge of the Troops now raising, & the Minute-Men with their Arms &c. £350,000; these added together will make an enormous Sum, & there are several Charges still behind; such as the Voluntier Compys at Williamsburg, the Payment of the Members of the Convention &c." There were no taxes coming in, and for a time the solution seemed to be the issuance of paper money based on a vague promise of eventual redemption in hard money.

Insofar as his family was affected by the war, Mason was not anxious to see his older sons tramping off to the sound of fife and drum. "My Son George may perhaps have a Mind to enter into the Service," Mason told a close friend and neighbor, "in which Case, pray tell him that it will be very contrary to my Inclination, & that I advise him by all Means against it. When the Plan for the Minute-Men is compleated, if he has a Mind to enter into that I shall have no Objection; as I look upon it to be the true natural, and safest Defence of this, or any other free Country; & as such, wish to see it encouraged to the utmost." Young George was 22 and not well—not up to the rigors of regular duty anyway—and in his search for better health he was a frequent visitor at the medicinal baths in Augusta County. William Mason was 18 and wanted his share of military glory, but Thomson (16), John (9), and Thomas (5) were too young for anything more than wooden swords and charges up and down the slopes of Gunston Hall.

As usual, Mason was unwell in the Richmond heat and had to miss some Convention sessions. When not ailing, however, Mason could be a dynamo of energy. He sidestepped the appointment to Congress despite the urging of Henry and Jefferson. "But my getting clear of this Appointment has avail'd me little," he confided, "as I have been since, in Spite of every thing I could do to the Contrary, put upon the Committee of Safety; which is even more inconvenient & disagreeable to me than going to Congress." This committee was charged with carrying on the functions of government while Lord Dunmore was afloat at the mouth of the York River, attempting to suppress colonial resistance. The Convention committee would leave local concerns to the county committees, but somebody needed the authority to buy huge quantities of powder, hundreds of muskets, and order blankets, tents, fodder, dried beef, flints, salt, sails, and all the items suddenly grown dear in a wartime economy. Mason saw the job was extraordinarily demanding and asked his colleagues not to load him with such chores, "but was answer'd by an universal NO."

Thus Mason took on some of the duties of a quartermaster-general and inspector-general. Despite all Mason's excuses, his fellow delegates respected his capacity for work, while his personal integrity was beyond question. By Mason's standards it was one thing to try and sell perhaps a hundred thousand pounds of prime tobacco before the prices tumbled, and quite another to take more than a farthing he was due from the public treasury. His long service as a Truro Parish vestryman and Fairfax County justice of the peace (an important, powerful post in the eighteenth century) had provided Mason many opportunities to handle the funds of others. He was as careful with the parish money when building a brick wall around the church as he was when spending his own pounds sterling for an addition to

Gunston Hall. Mason's reputation for thoroughness and honesty therefore overcame his protests when public duties needed tending.

Moreover, there was a humane side to Mason that others came to understand as part of his greatness. After war broke out the loyalty of dozens of British subjects in the Virginia mercantile trade was questioned. These were traders and store-keepers sent to Virginia by large houses in Glasgow, Edinburgh, and London whose allegiance was to their ledgers and to no particular flag. Mason knew this and was sympathetic to their difficulties. He drafted a loyalty oath and prefaced it with enough anti-British propaganda to satisfy the most zealous patriot. "Whereas the long premeditated and now avowed Design of the British Ministry to force Loyal Colonists into an abject surrender of their Rights and Priveleges as Freeman, are still persisted in by the British Government," it was necessary for the colonists to act the part of free men. The colonists found it necessary "by an Appeal to Heaven, to enter into a more firm Union for our common defence, and to distinguish those deserving our Protection from such as are Enemies to our just Cause."

Mason's oath was to be sworn by all freemen over sixteen and contained a promise to observe the non-importation association as well as a vow not to "take up Arms against the good People Freemen Inhabitants of this Colony or any other part of America acting under & in support of the Ordinances of general Convention during the unhappy differences now subsisting between Great Britain and America." Those who took the oath also were to swear that they would not "directly or indirectly by correspondence, Signs or Tokens or by any ways or means aid, assist, or support any Power that shall be emploied against the good People of America." Finally, the jurors (those who would take the oath) pledged that they would defend and support Virginia "against all Invasions & Insurrections whatsoever . . . So help me God."

The last provision was doubtless made with Governor Dunmore clearly in mind, for in the preamble Mason alluded to the royal appointee's "unexampled & wanton suspension of the Law of the Land . . . by seising, and imprisoning and transporting the persons of our peaceable Citizens, by declaring our Servants and Slaves free and inviting & arming them to assassinate their Masters, our innocent Wives and helpless Children, which cruel and horrid Measures have been countenanced & supported by some wicked Persons among ourselves." Dunmore was detested with a special kind of hatred reserved for any man who raised the bloody banner of slave rebellion, and any natives of Great Britain who wanted to stay at large in Virginia had to make it clear that they would do nothing to aid John Murray, fourth Earl of Dunmore.

No doubt the law was not meant to bring every citizen before a committee of safety, but only those suspicious characters who refused to take such an oath. Confronted persons who would not swear their loyalty were to be hauled before a local committee and fined. If they persisted in their refusal, heavier penalties were prescribed; and then there was always the most powerful but unstated punishment—tar and feathers from an impatient mob. Actually, there seems to have been little use of tar-and-feathers in Virginia as a "Tory converter," but the threat was ever present in towns, where pitch buckets were as handy as goose-down pillows. Said to have been a New-England invention, "the Art of tarring & feathering" was not so popular in the South as effigy-burning and newspaper lambasting.

To a gentleman of Mason's tastes and habits, the proper way to deal with Tories was the legal way—fines, test oaths, and deportation. Hence he drafted an oath that was worded "such as no good Man wou'd object to" and the Richmond merchants "declare themselves well pleased with it." After some debate, however, Mason's oath was tabled; but its effect came through in a resolution which called upon Virginians "to treat all natives of *Great Britain*, resident here, as do not show themselves enemies to the common cause of *America*, with lenity and friendship." (In fact, committees of safety did hold certain aliens under surveillance, and by 1777 a test oath was adopted by the Virginia legislature.)

At last the Convention of 1775 finished its business and Mason hurried from Shockoe Hill, in little Richmond to Hanover Court-House, then on to Bowling Green in Caroline County, and finally to his own ferry across the Occoquan and so back to Gunston Hall. Once home he wrote Washington a full account of the business that the general had missed:

> During the first Part of the Convention Partys run so high, that we had frequently no other Way of preventing improper Measures but by Procrastination, urging the previous Question, & giving Men time to reflect; however after some Weeks, the Bablers were pretty well silenced, a few weighty Members began to take the Lead, several wholsome Regulations were made, and if the Convention

41

had continued to sit a few Days longer, I think the public Safety wou'd have been as well provided for as our present Circumstances permit.

Mason had long been a militia colonel but the title had been more honorary than anything. Now, with a full-scale war in prospect, he was pleased to tell Washington of the Convention plan to raise "8,000 good Troops, ready for Action, & composed of men in whose Hands the Sword may be safely trusted."

A tax bill was passed but collections deferred for two years (Virginians did not mind taxes, so long as they were not collected), and another convention was to meet a year hence, with the delegates to be elected in the intervening months. "The Part we have to act at present seems to require our laying in good Magazines [of weapons], training our people, & having a good Number of them ready for action," Mason explained to Washington. On the whole, Mason was pleased with the way things had gone at Richmond.

There was one disturbing element in the Virginia situation which worried Mason and which he hoped the Minute Men plan might solve. This was the presence of Lord Dunmore in Chesapeake Bay or off Norfolk with a raiding squadron of British men o'war. "Many of the principal Familys are removing from Norfolk, Hampton, York & Williamsburg, occasioned by the Behaviour of Lord Dunmore," Mason reported to Washington. In the years ahead, Gunston Hall was to be the scene of more than one evacuation as British naval vessels freely roamed the bay and once went up the Potomac as far as Alexandria.

These worries were in the future, however, and in 1775 Mason believed the defense of Virginia was proceeding efficiently. He was probably surprised when a committee of Alexandria merchants became alarmed in December 1775 and urged him to greater action. Frightened by Dunmore's depredations, the merchants said that "daily Experience evinces, that the Minute System is very inadequate to the Design; wherever the Colony is expos'd and vulnerable" as at Alexandria, "there we wou'd recommend Regular Forces to be station'd." The alarmed business men, aware that their investments were threatened, also urged "your promoting the fitting out a few Vessells of War, to protect the Bay & Rivers, from Lord Dunmore's Pirates." As often happens when men of commerce become frightened, the Alexandria merchants tended to overreact to rumors of invasion. "The Sword is drawn, the Bayonet is allready at our Breasts, therefore some immediate Effort is necessary to ward off the meditated Blow," they pleaded.

A report that a British spy had planned to rendezvous with Dunmore at Alexandria in the spring of 1776 had perhaps touched off the merchants' alarm. To help calm his friends and make a show of public activity, Mason and John Dalton joined with the Maryland Committee of Safety in ordering a small fleet of row galleys that were to carry light canon—not very effective against a British ship of the line but a comforting sight to relieved citizens who believed rumors of slave revolts and sneak attacks from Dunmore's imposing ships.

The first dogwood blossoms in the spring of 1776 made northern Virginia seem too pleasant a place for anything warlike to occur, but Mason heard reports that the British had evacuated Boston and were headed southward. Mason listened to the stories and made his own—and as it turned out—a partially correct judgment. "I am very unable to judge of military Affairs; but it appears to me that if Genl. Howe acts the Part of a wise Man, & an experienced Officer, he will . . . retire to Hallifax, give his Troops a little time, by Ease & Refreshment, to recover their Spirits, & be in Readiness, as soon as the Season permits, to relieve Quebec," he wrote Washington.

An American victory at Moore's Creek, North Carolina, coupled with the British withdrawal from Boston, had buoyed the patriots's hopes, Mason reported, and the supply and troop situation in Maryland and Virginia was improved. Amidst all the activity, Mason fondly recalled the days when he stood on the porch at Mount Vernon. "I fancy myself under your hospitable Roof at Mount Vernon and lay aside Reserve. May God grant us a return to those halcyon Days; when every Man may sit down at his Ease under the Shade of his own Vine, & his own fig-tree, & enjoy the Sweets of domestic Life! Or if this is too much, may He be pleased to inspire us with spirit & resolution, to bear our present & future Sufferings, becoming Men determined to transmit to our Posterity, unimpair'd, the Blessings we have received from our Ancestors!"

Mason was not carried away too often, but as he said, when he remembered those pleasant hours at Mount Vernon it was easy to become rhetorical. Washington responded by asking his old friend to do a favor and help settle an estate for his wife's family. The war went on and everybody guessed where the British would suddenly appear, but Mason had been half right—Howe took his army to Halifax, Nova

Scotia, for refitting, and bided his moment for a new landing on the mainland.

The newspapers carried rumors to Baltimore and Williamsburg, where there were two *Virginia Gazettes* and four sets of opinions. There were radicals ready to leave the British empire, moderates who hoped to stay (but at no cost), conservatives who were ready to concede Parliament a theoretical right to regulate commerce but no taxing power, and arch-conservatives who wanted to go back to the *status quo ante bellum*—even if it meant paying crown taxgatherers. The last group finally left the colony or kept their mouths shut and their doors barred, while those in the center tended to let the radicals lead the colony toward a bold position.

Placing Mason in the company of radicals seems out of character, yet he found himself agreeing more often with Jefferson and Henry and less with the Braxtons, Nicholases, and other hesitant Virginians. "Old men were seldom warm Whigs," the contemporary historian David Ramsay noted; "they could not relish the changes which were daily taking place, attached to ancient forms and habits, they could not readily accommodate themselves to new systems. Few of the very rich were active in forwarding the revolution. This was remarkably the case in the eastern and middle states; but the reverse took place in the southern extreme of the confederacy. There were in no part of America more determined Whigs than the opulent slaveholders in Virginia, the Carolinas, and Georgia."

Mason was the exemplary figure in this latter category—and his conduct was all the more remarkable when the risks are considered. In other words, the cobbler in Boston who became a radical was risking, at the most, his tools and his trade but no great wealth. The southern plantation owners were vulnerable to attack because many of them lived (as did Mason) on deep navigable streams which the British navy could ply; and their homes were in constant jeopardy, along with their furniture, silverware, wine cellars, clocks, glassware, money and, as they saw it—their lives. Yet they were a rather determined lot, and in George Mason we see the patriarch of those radicals whose dreams and perseverance led to the founding of a nation.

A radical Mason never knew had great popularity early in 1776: Thomas Paine. During the winter of 1775-1776 the impact of Paine's pamphlet, *Common Sense*, had struck at the root of American loyalty to George III. Until that time, the blame for the Americans' troubles had been placed on the "evil, designing, wicked British ministry." Now Paine tore the image of George III as a benign, fatherly sovereign to shreds:

> In England a king hath little more to do than to make war and give away places; which in plain terms is to impoverish the nation and set it together by the ears. A pretty business indeed for a man to be allowed eight hundred thousand sterling a year for, and worshipped into the bargain! Of more worth is one honest man to society, and in the sight of God, than all the crowned ruffians that ever lived.

That was pretty strong stuff for the colonists, but Paine had struck the right chord. In a few months the notion that a man could be a king because of an accident of birth seemed childish nonsense to men who a few years earlier had yearned for an invitation to the king's birthday ball in Williamsburg. When the freeholders of Fairfax County returned Mason to the Convention called for May 1776, the climate of opinion had made a radical shift. Washington wrote Joseph Reed of Philadelphia that Americans were reluctant to think of a complete break with England, "but time and persecution bring many wonderful things to pass; and by private letters, which I have lately received from Virginia, I find 'Common Sense' is working a powerful change there in the minds of many men."

And so it had, for Richard Henry Lee and Jefferson were in the Continental Congress and ready to throw the weight of the Virginia delegation behind any movement toward independence. John Adams, their colleague from Massachusetts, looked round the halls of Congress and wished mightily for a groundswell of opinion so that all ties with England would be ripped asunder. "The management of so complicated and mighty a machine as the United Colonies," Adams observed, "requires the meekness of Moses, the patience of Job, and the wisdom of Solomon, added to the valour of David." In 1776 the Virginia Convention found all of the Biblical characteristics united in George Mason.

Chapter V

"A Time to Rend"

"After a smart fit of Gout," Mason reported to Richard Henry Lee, "which detain'd me at Home the first of the Session, I have at last reached this Place, where, to my great Satisfaction, I find the first grand Point has been carried nem: con."

From his writing desk in Williamsburg Mason thus reported to Lee that the convention of 1776 had seen fit to cut its last ties with England "nem: con."—unanimously. "The opponents being so few, that they did not think fit to divide, or contradict the general Voyce." So Mason had arrived too late for the first great question but he was ready to go to work. Meanwhile, Lee and Jefferson had been busy in the Congress at Philadelphia, and on May 10 the resolution urging colonies to adopt a constitutional government conducive "to the happiness and safety of their constituents in particular, and America in general," had been approved. So all the steps preliminary to a final break with England had been taken, and while the formalities were still to be worked out, the United Colonies were no longer part of the British Empire—except on the maps in English schoolrooms.

Once Mason was able to ride a horse, after the swelling in his pain-racked body subsided, he had tried to make up for his absence at the first week of the Convention. He doubtless took the so-called "Burgesses Route" from Gunston Hall and probably rode at an easy pace, accompanied by a black servant and a packhorse laden with a change of linen, proper vests and coats, shaving equipment, and an extra empty chest. Except for gnats and horseflies, the trip could be pleasant in early May, when cardinals darted from oak and pine boughs and even the distant calls of a crow seemed welcome. On this trip Mason had much to ponder besides the beauties of nature, for the consensus in public and private discussions was all too plain. The connection with England was at an end, so the proper question was, "What next?"

Perhaps Mason used the trip to Williamsburg to sound out friends as to what they expected from the Convention. As he moved southeastward, there were wayside plantations where the doors were never bolted. A late supper meant that news, gossip, and opinion could be mingled with a friendly glass. In ordinary times the talk would shift from tobacco prices to horseflesh, and then to local politics, and back to horses. But in the spring of 1776 the main topic of discussion was where the British intended to land once they left Halifax, and what the Virginians intended to do about their royal connection. Although Mason was still on the high road to Williamsburg when the Convention declared that the colonies were no longer under George III's protection and ought to be free and independent, there was that slight matter of implementation.

As Mason told Lee, the delegates were preoccupied with "the most important of all Subjects—Government." A committee had been appointed to prepare a Constitution and a Declaration of Rights, and as Mason noted the group was, "according to Custom, overcharged with useless members. . . . We shall, in all probability have a thousand ridiculous and impracticable proposals, & of Course, a Plan form'd of hetrogenious, jarring & unintelligible Ingredients."

The only way to make any progress in such circumstances, Mason reasoned, was for "a few Men of Integrity & Abilitys, whose Countrys Interest lies next their Hearts, undertaking this Business." With Lee's brother, Thomas Ludwell Lee, as an aide Mason let it be known that he had thought about the business at hand and was prepared to submit a draft to aid the committee in its work. Edmund Pendleton wrote Jefferson a few days after Mason took charge of the committee: "The Political Cooks are busy in preparing the dish, and as Colo Mason seems to have the Ascendancy in the great work, I have Sanguine hopes it will be framed so as to Answer it's end, Prosperity to the Community and Security to Individuals, but I am yet a stranger to the Plan." Another delegate thought "the great business will go on well, as I think there will be no great difference of opinion among our best speakers, Henry, Mason, Mercer, Dandridge, Smith, and I am apt to think the President will concur with them in sentiment."

Young James Madison, down from Orange County for his first term of public service, was added to the committee and saw at once how the more experienced legislators moved confidently.

47

Thomas Ludwell Lee was pleased with the May 10 resolution and thought the business of establishing "a just and equal government would not perhaps be so very difficult." Patrick Henry was not so sure. "Perhaps I'm mistaken, but I fear too great a Byass to Aristocracy prevails. . . . And to see those who have so fatally advised us, still guiding, or at least sharing our public counsels, alarms me," Henry told Richard Henry Lee.

Henry's fears were like many of the spellbinder's anxieties— ill-founded. For Mason's intellectual resources were, in contrast to his bodily pains, at their very peak. A lifetime of reading in law books, in Locke, Sidney, Machiavelli, Montesquieu, *Cato's Letters,* and other handbooks of political theory had given Mason a sharp understanding of what a republican society had to offer its citizens. With the old forms of the Glorious Revolution in England as his model, the committeemen listened in appreciation and nodded approval as Mason reported. "That all Men are born equally free and independent, and have certain inherent natural Rights," Mason began, "among which are the Enjoyment of Life and Liberty, with the Means of acquiring and possessing Property, and pursueing and obtaining Happiness and Safety."

Mason ticked off the rights freemen were due, one by one. All power was vested in the people, and their elected representatives were bound to serve the common good. Whenever a government failed to offer its citizens "the greatest Degree of Happiness and Safety," the people had a right "to reform, alter or abolish it." No citizen was entitled to special or hereditary privileges. The government ought to have three separate and distinct branches—legislative, judicial, and executive—and offices were best filled when public men were "at fixed Periods . . . reduced to a private Station, and returned, by frequent, certain and regular Elections, into that Body from which they were taken." The holding of property was a right not to be infringed, nor denied any citizen, except by due process of law. Accused persons were to know the nature of charges against them, and have counsel, and be entitled to a speedy and fair jury trial in the vicinity of the accusation; nor could "he be compelled to give Evidence against himself." No citizen was to be arrested without a legal warrant, and ex post facto laws were to be avoided. "The press, being the great bulwark of Liberty, can never be restrained but in a despotic government." Religion was a matter of "Reason and Conviction, not . . . Force or Violence; and therefore . . . all Men shou'd enjoy the fullest Toleration in the Exercise of Religion, according to the Dictates of Conscience."

Edmund Randolph, another young member present, who observed more than the older, busier delegates, was to recall the Mason report almost with reverence. The drafts submitted by Mason, Randolph later noted, "swallowed up all the rest, by fixing the grounds and plan, which after great discussion and correction, were finally ratified." In the committee of the whole house, the draft was treated with general approval except by one or two conservatives. Momentarily, Thomas Ludwell Lee turned from optimism to gloom, reporting that the Convention had abruptly stumbled "at the threshold. . . . We find such difficulty in laying the foundation stone, that I very much fear for that Temple to Liberty which was proposed to be erected thereon." The trouble was, Lee explained, that "a certain set of Aristocrats, for we have such monsters here, finding that their execrable system cannot be reared on such foundations, have to this time kept us at Bay on the first line, which declares all men to be born equally free and independent." A line-by-line debate on the Declaration of Rights was the last thing Mason and his supporters wanted. Yet Robert Carter Nicholas, a respected but reactionary man, had insisted that the first line might encourage a civil war for, if slaves were involved, would they be considered "born equally free and independent"?

Without intending to raise a storm, perhaps, Nicholas had struck at the Achilles heel of the American Revolution. For in fact there was a double standard of freedom that the Americans were applying—and had applied since the first arguments in 1765. As some Englishmen had with consistency pointed out, it was unique to hear slaveholding Americans complain over the threats of inequality and injustice. Of course, it was an inconsistency without resolution, and to get around Nicholas's embarrassing question the radicals answered that slaves were not considered "constituent members" of society, and thus no abstract maxim on freedom could apply to the blacks.

From the twentieth century we look back with hindsight and regret this sophistry as tragic, but in the context of the times by which men must be judged, the notion of freedom for *all* men was beyond their comprehension. Thus the Revolution fell short of our expectations, but in nearly every other respect it not only met the hopes of the generations then living but of what Mason himself alluded to as "Generations unborn."

When the committee finished going over Mason's draft of the Declaration of Rights, a printed copy found its way into Dixon and Hunter's *Virginia Gazette* of June 1. Postriders soon carried the issue north and south, so that in a matter of weeks newspaper readers along the Atlantic seaboard were reading Mason's words. Their impact was evident. After the haggling in Williamsburg ended, the Convention joined the Declaration with Mason's version of a Constitution, and in less than two months both documents had become law. As John Adams told Henry, "we all look up to Virginia for examples," and here were examples indeed.

The example that newspapers spread across the land was not the final version of the Declaration of Rights, but except for one notable alteration the emerging sixteen articles were a distillation of the English common law, American usage, and common sense. The exception was James Madison's suggested changing of the article on religion from "the fullest toleration of the exercise of religion" to a much broader phrase. At Madison's suggestion, the revised article held that "all men are equally entitled to the free exercise of religion, according to the dictates of conscience." This change was a salutary one, although Mason looked back a few years later and thought some of the last-minute emendations "not for the better." In the same breath, however, Mason noted that his work had been "closely imitated by all the other States"—which was only a slight exaggeration.

Scholars and politicians have since marveled at the speed which the Virginia Convention exhibited—but revolutions often culminate in the space of a few weeks when the tensions of generations are finally relieved. So Mason did not pause in self-congratulation but sped on with the main business—a constitution that would furnish Virginia with a vehicle to carry on government. What kind of a government? Clearly it must be a republican form, with the people represented in a legislative body, and the main difference from the old royal form was that, as Mason noted in his Declaration, "That Power is, by God and Nature, vested in, and consequently derived from the People." With that principle as "the Pole-Star" of his plan, Mason well remembered his readings, particularly in Montesquieu and Lecke. He had a few other guides, including a tract John Adams gave Richard Henry Lee, Lee's own ideas in essay form, and Jefferson's draft of a constitution which had been whipped out in Philadelphia in anticipation of the swift movement of events in Williamsburg. But the main model for

Mason's constitution was the 150 years of experience Virginians had acquired in self-government.

The first draft of Mason's plan maintained the old trapping of the political structure with a two-house General Assembly, an executive branch consisting of a governor and privy council, and a judiciary wing with an attorney-general and various courts of law and admiralty. Essentially, Mason's plan was conservative in that the members of the lower house had to be 24 years old and own lands worth £1,000, while members of the upper house would qualify only if 28 and owned £2,000 in real property. Voting for these offices was to be fairly democratic, however, in that just about any white male who leased or owned land or "hath been the father of three children" while residing in Virginia was considered qualified.

Elections were to be held annually for the lower house but the governor had a three-year term and the upper house was to serve four years (and then be ineligible for another four). Most of the power was lodged in the lower house, where appropriations would be made and appointments initiated, but the executive could appoint the locally powerful justicies of the peace. What Mason seems to have had in mind was a government almost like the old royal system except that there was no veto power over laws enacted by the legislature, and all the taxes were raised and spent either in Virginia or at the legislature's bidding.

Another two or three weeks were required before the final draft of the Virginia Constitution was ready for approval, but in essence the first plan offered by Mason was to be the model for state government in the Old Dominion until 1830. Jefferson's draft had been sent to Williamsburg in the charge of his law professor at William and Mary, George Wythe. Jefferson's plan had a bill of rights (much of it overlapping the Mason draft) and a three-branch government, but its general tone was more liberal than Virginians in that day were ready to practice. Both men wanted offices rotated, with most of the power lodged in the lower house, but Jefferson's ideas on prohibiting captial punishment ("for any crime, excepting murder") and slavery were too much for the average Virginian to stomach. However, the immediate value of Jefferson's work was that his preamble to the proposed constitution was easily copied for his draft of the Declaration of Independence—as a justification for the Revolution against George III.

The Convention, eager to get on with its chief concern, was

disposed to take Mason's plan "lock, stock, and barrel." All of the laws passed by colonial legislatures were left undisturbed. The whole emphasis was on orderly and minimal change, with the people substituted for the crown as the ultimate authority. Later, Jefferson and Madison were to see "capital defects" in the plan, but at the time it was obvious that Mason's thoughts were reflecting the consensus of the Virginians who were in charge of the Revolution.

Notice that as Virginia broke its imperial tie the new designation was that of a commonwealth—another carryover from the Glorious Revolution. Mason's Declaration of Rights and Constitution were rooted in the English theory of resistance to tyrants as a natural, indefeasible right *and duty*. If we want to understand why Mason became so heavily involved in the War for Independence, the only explanation that makes much sense is Mason's strong sense of duty to his country (that is, Virginia) and to his family. His ancestors in Staffordshire had been involved in a revolution because of *their* duty, and Mason was reluctant to follow the same route except that the alternative was unthinkable—a risk of losing life, liberty, and property.

When Mason explained what had happened in the Convention, he was inclined to give much of the credit to the people. While certain Englishmen were trying to create the impression that the Revolution was fomented by "a Junto of ambitious Men against the Sense of the People of America," Mason wrote a relative, "On the Contrary, nothing has been done without the Approbation of the People, who have indeed out run their Leaders; so that no capital Measure hath been adopted, until they called loudly for it." Within two years' time, Mason was able to report that the Declaration of Rights and Constitution had satisfied Virginians so well that "the People become every Day more & more attach'd to it; and I trust that neither the Power of Great Britain, nor the Power of Hell will be able to prevail against it."

Whatever the devil tried to do is conjecture, but the British ministry tried to topple the Virginia Constitution and all the others that followed. Within the next few year seven states or would-be states had borrowed liberally from Mason's Declaration of Rights in forming their own, and in the two centuries since Mason wearily copied his draft the ripples from the Virginia document have extended around the globe. The Virginia Convention had pointed the way for other colonies-turned-states by placing their fundamental law in explicit, written form.

The much-praised British Constitution existed only in a vague conglomerate of laws and customs, but Mason and his associates had created what Edmund Randolph explained as "a standing ark, to which first principles can be brought on a test." Much of the talk about a government of laws, and not of men, rested on the principle that a permanent constitution which all citizens could understand would protect them from arbitary power. When he wrote a history of the stirring events of 1776, Randolph observed that two main objects were in sight when the Declaration of Rights was authorized by the Convention. One purpose was "that the legislature should not in their acts violate any of those canons; the other, that in all revolutions of time, of human opinion, and of government, a perpetual standard should be erected, around which the people might rally, and by a notorious record be forever admonished to be watchful, firm and virtuous."

All that remained for the convention delegates was to turn the reins of power over to the new government. "Everything which had been done in the Convention of May [1776] was hailed as masterpieces of political wisdom and acted upon with a cheerfulness and submission," Randolph recalled. "The young boasted that they were treading upon the republican ground of Greece and Rome and contracted a sovereign contempt for British institutions." Patrick Henry was chosen as the state's first governor and took office one day after the final knot with England was severed. The delegates returned home, committed to maintaining order and carrying on the war until the regular wheels of government would commence turning with the October session of the newly created General Assembly. That empty chest which Mason must have brought down from Gunston Hall now went back, no doubt full of books, dog-eared committee reports, and newspapers with full accounts of the momentous session.

The times were memorable, indeed. As the Bible advised,

> To every thing there is a season, and a time to every purpose under the heaven. A time to be born, and a time to die; a time to plant, and a time to pluck up that which is planted. A time to kill, and a time to heal; a time to break down, and a time to build up. A time to weep, and a time to laugh; a time to mourn, and a time to dance. . . . A time to rend, and a time to sew.

53

These words from Ecclesiastes may have been in the minds of the delegates as they turned homeward. The time for revolt had come and with it a season for change; and the war would bring killing and dying and weeping, but there would also be a time to build.

Mason was to be impatient with later claims that the Americans had always intended to rend the royal tie—that the protests of 1765 had only been a feint in the real battle for complete independence. "The Assertion that Independence was originally designed here," he insisted in a letter to England, was completely untrue; but by 1778 "things have gone such Lengths, that it is a Matter of Moonshine to us, whether Independence was at first intended. . . . The truth is, we have been forced into it, as the only means of self-preservation, to guard our County & posterity from the greatest of all Evils, such another infernal Government (if it deserves the Name of Government) as the Provinces groaned under, in the latter Ages of the Roman Commonwealth." In a word—despotism. George Mason forgot his gout and his cramped living quarters and the long ride to Williamsburg for a special purpose. Neither he nor his nine children would ever live in a land where all the rules of the game were dictated by men 3,000 miles away.

Chapter VI

A Matter of Endurance & Providence

WHATEVER wishes Mason felt for a retirement from public life were suppressed for the next few years as the fortunes of war waxed and waned. The new state's constitution made a general committee of safety unnecessary, but there was much to be done before the Northern Neck would be secure from British threats. The British had shelled and burned several coastal towns, and although Dunmore was finally driven away, there was still a chance that a single 20-gun British man o'war could sweep up the Potomac and devastate estates and villages along the way. Mason took his duties as an ordnance master seriously as he sent messages to neighboring committees of safety and to the Continental Congress, begging for more gunpowder, for cannon that could be used in an earthwork battery to defend Alexandria, and for salt to pack the meat needed by hungry soldiers.

There was good reason for alarm, since William Brent's house in Stafford County had been burned by a British shore party that could as easily have moved on Gunston Hall. Mason was torn between his desire to have property protected by a regular force, mounted and watchful, instead of the minute-men who were widely dispersed and hard to summon if a British dreadnaught appeared. In general Mason believed that standing armies were expensive, wasteful, and anti-democratic; but the alternative in wartime was even more forbidding, and the potential harm a company of British regular troops might wreak was to be avoided at all costs.

There is a story, probably apocryphal, that Mason was warned in the summer of 1776 that British troops were marauding on Aquia Creek, not far from Gunston Hall, and that Mason sent his family fleeing deep into the Northern Neck after warning Martha

Washington that she should join them. Even if true, Mason himself probably stayed on at his mansion to protect the great house. By the rules of war, still followed during the Revolution, armies were not to molest or damage private property unless it was used by the enemy for some military purpose. We can be fairly sure that whenever rumors of British ships on the Potomac reached Gunston Hall, Mason made certain that every weapon above a kitchen knife went out of sight, along with the silver plate, best wines, and whatever cash Mason had on hand.

Predictably, Mason was elected a delegate to the first session of the House of Delegates, but he was in no hurry to return to Duke of Gloucester Street in Williamsburg while there was so much talk of trouble on Queen Street in Alexandria. The British had finally made their move on Long Island, swept Washington's army back, and the tide of war seemed running in their direction when the first frosts covered the fields around Gunston Hall. The golden and red hues of the surrounding forest made a serene setting for the worrisome business of granting safe-conduct passes to harmless loyalists, but as a justice of the peace Mason also had the more pleasant duty of signing marriage certificates.

The news from the North was good and bad. Washington's army was still intact, but if Howe bestirred himself that was no guessing as to how long the hard-pressed Continentals could hold out. Still, from his command post at Harlem Heights, Washington had time to turn his thoughts back to Fairfax County. "Remember me to all our neighbors and friends, particularly to Colo. Mason, to whom I could write if I had time to do it fully and satisfactorily," Washington told his farm manager.

Besides Washington's danger, Mason's role in the war seemed tame indeed. When Mason ran out of excuses he finally headed for Williamsburg, arrived late for the session, and gave an adequate excuse so that he was not fined for his tardiness. He promptly offered the House a petition from the residents of Alexandria seeking state aid in their projected harbor defense and was able to report that a bill passed allowing the town funds for two militia infantry companies and one artillery unit, to be paid "only when upon duty" at bi-weekly drills and on guard duty. Other military business which took Mason's attention included authorization for a cavalry force that was to be raised by the commonwealth for duty with Washington.

Taxes, weapons, and food supplies seemed to cause most of the problems of the session, although one domestic difficulty had Mason's full attention. Since the Declaration of Rights promised Virginians the free exercise of religion, the dissenters in their midst now demanded their full share of the newly proclaimed freedom. The Anglican church was still supported by public taxes and only marriages solemnized by Anglican ministers were recognized as legal. Depending on the vigilance or vindictiveness or laxity of local authorities, dissenting preachers could be ignored, tolerated or jailed. In Culpeper County, the Rev. Elijah Craig had been imprisoned twice for preaching from a Baptist pulpit, and there were other instances of persecution that showed old scores were unsettled.

Mason sympathized with the dissenters and had some of the burden left on his shoulders because Jefferson was still in Congress and Madison was inexperienced. Mason was not prepared to go as far as Madison in his liberalism toward religious dissent, but the harassment of preachers and God-fearing laymen was to Mason inexcusable. He offered a resolution to the House exempting dissenters from payments to the Anglican church and sought the suspension of any law that made persecutions for "any Opinions in Matter of Religion . . . or the exercising any Mode of worship whatsoever."

Mason eventually came to share the extremely liberal views of Madison and Jefferson on religious freedom, and after the war he was a champion for the renowned Virginia law establishing that precious right.

Meanwhile, the Continental army and the British forces went into winter quarters, a lucky circumstance for the Americans since Howe's army was strong enough to have pushed Washington into a corner had Sir William been more zealous. The breathing spell brought pressure on the Virginia legislature to help Washington with recruits and food, and Mason seems to have had a hand in the main business during the rest of the 1776 session. Mason was also appointed to a committee for revising the code of Virginia along with Jefferson, George Wythe, Edmund Pendleton, and Thomas Ludwell Lee. Lee and Mason were not lawyers but so well-read that they were logical choices for the group, which was charged with sweeping all the royal cobwebs out of the state statute books. Mason was assigned to a revision of the criminal law and acts dealing with land, "but if he finds it too much, the other Gentlemen will take off his Hands any part he pleases," he noted. How much Mason contributed to the revisors' work is uncertain, except that he did help with the land statutes. The three lawyers understandably wound up with most of the chore.

Upon his return to Fairfax County Mason plunged back into the work of the committee of safety, buying more powder and provisions. His income had been hit by the war, of course, but in one sense Gunston Hall was almost a self-contained community, so that the Masons and their slaves ate well and among the younger members of the family the chief concern was probably who had to be a British officer or redcoat in their sham battles outside the hedge-rowed gardens. Mason tried to develop a market for tobacco in the French West Indies and probably turned some tobacco fields into wheat and maize, knowing that cereals and fodder would be needed by the army. Then a small-pox inoculation laid Mason low in the summer of 1777 and he could not attend the House of Delegates session, a circumstance that did not stop his colleagues from nominating him to serve on their delegation to the Continental Congress.

Non-plussed by this vote of confidence, Mason begged off. "Return my thanks to the Assembly for the honor they have been pleased to do me," Mason wrote the Speaker of the House, but he had to plead hardship and decline the appointment. "My own domestic affairs are so circumstanced as not to admit of my continued absence from home, where a numerous family of children calls for my constant attention; nor do I think I have a right to vacate my seat in the house of delegates, without the consent of my constituents; and such of them as I have had the opportunity of consulting are adverse to it." Mason escaped the duty, but not all of his neighbors were pleased.

Washington finally almost lost patience with Mason's excuses and lamented "the fatal policy too prevalent in most of the states, of employing their ablest Men at home in posts of honor or profit" while the national government languished. "Where are our Men of abilities? Why do they not come forth to save their Country? Let this voice my dear Sir call upon you—Jefferson & others—do not from a mistaken opinion that we are about to set down under our own Vine and our own fig tree let our hitherto noble struggle end in Ignominy," Washington pleaded. Mason was deaf to this call upon his patriotism, however, for no man seemed to love his own hearthside more or dread a trip away from familiar byways more than Mason. Much as he admired Washington, Mason's resolution to stay away from the halls of Congress was final.

When Mason returned to the House of Delegates in the fall of 1777 he was determined to do something about the unsettled western lands. Technically, Virginia owned all the land (or had a royal title, anyway) in the Ohio valley and on to the tip of the Great Lakes. To secure this claim by a military venture, Mason joined with Wythe, Jefferson, and Henry in secret sessions with George Rogers Clark at Williamsburg. They authorized Clark to raise a force in Kentucky and strike at British outposts in the Illinois country. Mason doubtless wanted the country conquered for the blow it would deal the British, but he could not have been uninterested in the western land claims he owned which would be on more solid footing if Clark's expedition succeeded. After much hardship, Clark's small band did capture Kaskaskia and took the notorious "hair-buyer" Sir Henry Hamilton a prisoner; at Vincennes and Clark's letter reporting all this news to Mason of November 19, 1779, remains one of the great documents in western military literature.

The scope of Mason's interests at these legislative sessions was remarkable for both variety and the work-load. Impatient with committees, Mason seems to have often undertaken heavy assignments and worked late hours to finish single-handedly a job, thereby avoiding any wrangling over petty details. His bills in the critical session of 1777-1778, when the British had Washington penned up at Valley Forge, ranged from regulations on small-pox inoculations to punishment for gambling.

One of the most important pieces of legislation he ever attempted was written at this session in cooperation with Jefferson. Their bill "for adjusting & settling the Titles of Claimers of unpatented Lands under the former Government," was an attempt to open up the West to settlers and also to use frontier land sales to finance the war. In some ways the act failed on both counts, but it was in the execution and not in the intent that the law fell down. Mason and Jefferson wanted to give bona fide settlers a chance to own lands at low prices, and even went so far as to allow squatters up to 400 acres at dirt-cheap prices. But the law bogged down because of survey squabbles and the tricks of speculators and others who used the liberal provisions to their own advantage.

Mason himself was victimized by surveyors who coveted his Kentucky lands (claimed under the headright system of granting 50 acres per immigrant, with the rights saleable and convertible on unsettled lands). In time Mason forwarded claims for nearly 70,000 western acres in redemption for his headrights, but the lawyers gained more than Mason out of the venture—which was still in the courts when Mason died thirteen years later.

With other delegates, Mason must have toasted news of the great American victory at Saratoga in the fall of 1777, and its aftermath, the signing of a Franco-American military alliance. The prospect of military assistance from their old enemies, the French, delighted those Virginians who had found the French West Indies an important substitute for the old commercial channels with England. "American Prospects brighten every Day," Mason observed in July 1778, as he believed that nothing "but the speedy Arrival of a strong British Squadron can save the Enemie's Fleet & Army at N. York."

In fact, Mason was almost afraid that the war might end suddenly. "I am clearly of Opinion that War is the present Interest of these United States. The Union is yet incompleat, & will be so, until the inhabitants of the Territory from Cape Briton to the Missis[s]ippi are included in it." Mason did not think Canada should be left in British hands, once the war was won, but seized by the United States along with Florida. "The possession of these two places wou'd save us more than half a Million a Year," Mason reasoned, because without these coastal supply points the British could not keep a naval squadron ranging along the coast and hence American commerce would be free and prosperous.

Mason had no doubt that America would win the war and he held that the stupidity of the British cabinet was an ace-in-the-hole for the United States. First, he said, he would drink a toast to their new ally, Louis XVI, and then offer his next to "long Life & Continuance in Office to the present British ministry." When news of American military defeats disheartened others, Mason seems to have remained optimistic because Lord North was still at the helm in England.

Indeed, it was becoming clear to all Americans and to a good many Englishmen by 1779 that no British general was ever going to destroy Washington's army—and so long as Washington had men in the field the War for Independence was in full tilt. Mason was convinced that the longer the war lasted the more Americans would become prejudiced against England, and this was all to the good because in the postwar era "we [will] become better reconciled to foreign Manners & Manufacturers." This would end the mercantilistic dependence of American upon England for commodity buyers and permit Virginia tobacco to be sold in the world market for the first time in over a century. Clearly one advantage Mason and other

Americans expected out of the war was higher prices for their farm commodities, once the war ended and the ports of Amsterdam, Cherbourg, Hamburg, and Copenhagen welcomed American products.

During these exciting days there is no doubt that Mason often dined in the Raleigh Tavern and other Williamsburg hostelries, and there the talk turned to all subjects that public men dote upon after a tiring day in legislative chambers . Because their letters are almost without humor, we have a tendency in our time to think that our Revolutionary forebears were stern men who hardly ever cracked a joke or laughed out loud. But we can be sure they did have a sense of humor, and at times a bawdy one.

Mason's troubles with the gout were no joke, of course, but he managed to tell a good story at election time, and when it came to tasting a choice bottle of claret he was able to stay at the table with a clear head and a good palate. Public drunkeness was considered shameful, but a card game was often the attraction at the Governor's Palace after a good meal. Until the capital was moved to Richmond in 1780 (against Mason's protests) the little village of Williamsburg came alive during the legislative sessions, and we can suspect that little Sally and Besty Mason waited for father to return with trinkets from the shops kept by Williamsburg merchants. If Mason chanced to visit the Carter's general store he could have bought "Spanish licorice, Ladies sticking plaister, Greenhow's tincture for the teeth," and perhaps a stock of the small blown-glass bottles little girls liked to keep in their dolls' parlors.

On the serious side—and Mason was usually on the serious side—the lawmakers decided a few days before Christmas 1778 that too much grain was going into ardent spirits and decreed that no more distilling of wheat or rye was to be permitted unless the grain first had been refused by a military commissary. The law seemed necessary because "the great quantity of grain consumed in the distilleries" had produced "the present alarming scarcity. "Apparently everybody was not worrying about the British and doing little else; nor were the merits of slaves forgotten by the legislature, as the slave Kitt was purchased from his master and made a free man by the General Assembly as a reward for informing authorities about a counterfeiting ring in Brunswick County.

Life had its dark side, too. The draft law which Mason had helped write and pass had caused trouble in some counties. There is something about military duty that has always rubbed some Americans the wrong way, and during the Revolution a riot broke out in Loudoun County when local officials tried to enforce the conscription laws. In fact, there were also large numbers of deserters wandering loose in Accomack County at about the same time, and the situation grew so bad that Governor Patrick Henry desperately suggested a general amnesty might be declared to wipe the slate clean, since there was not much the state could do otherwise. Quota systems, bounties in cash, and promises of free western lands helped with the recruiting when a sense of duty proved unavailing, but when Virginia promised Washington some 6,000 men in 1778, and only 716 showed up at the general's camp—it was apparent that the system had huge flaws.

Faced with these facts, Mason still hated to admit that the militia system was not the best way to raise an army in a republic. Unfortunately his oldest son was ailing and could not serve even as a minute-man in 1779, when Mason wrote Washington asking for introductory letters for George Mason, Jr., who was about to embark for Europe "to try the Effect of some of the southern Climates of Europe." Mason wanted letters for his son addressed to Lafayette (then temporarily in France) and Benjamin Franklin. Within a few weeks he had a gracious letter back from Washington enclosing them, as the general said, "as I wish for instances in which I can testify the sincerity of my regard for you."

Friends imposed on Mason, too. His brother, Thomson, lived at Strawberry Plain in Loudoun County and had to be a party to a messy business concerning a young officer captured at Fort Washington. Through some mixup, the lieutenant had not been exchanged for a British prisoner, as had many others taken at the fall of Fort Washington. "His Wife," Mason wrote "who is said to be a worthy Woman, & has a Number of small children, is exceedingly distressed by her Husband's long Captivity." Mason took up the lady's cause and asked Washington to find the missing officer and bring him back safely to Loudoun County. We cannot be certain that Lieutenant Smith was eventually exchanged, but Mason tried.

Still a fugitive from service in the Continental Congress, Mason went to Williamsburg in October 1779 for the last session of the General Assembly in the ancient capital. The supporters of a move of the capital argued that the inland town was not as subject to British attack and closer to the center of the state. Mason drafted bills to compensate citizens whose property the enemy had destroyed or damaged, and he became involved in the tricky business of seizing the estates of those British subjects who were classified as enemy aliens.

His work was suddenly slowed by "a severe Fit of Gout, which confined me eight or ten Days, & has reduced me lower than I have been these twenty Years. . . . I am not able to stand five Minutes at a time, & find myself fatigued, beyond Measure, by the Share which Necessity obliges me to bear in the public Business, since Mr. Jefferson (who is appointed Governor) has left the House." Important bills were being pushed "thro' our Butcher's Shambles, the Committee of the Whole House, [where] they will probably be mutilated mangled & chop'd to Pieces."

Still the work had to be done and Mason felt compelled to work hard at it. He was upset that Maryland had refused to ratify the Articles of Confederation, reportedly because of resentment of the western land claims of Virginia. Maryland had no western lands and it was said that rival land speculators had been talking with the Maryland delegates, hoping for a deal that would injure the Ohio Company claims which Mason deemed so important. Mason prepared a legal brief to clarify the Virginia claims to lands below the Ohio, since a cession to the United States of the upper Ohio Valley was in the wind. Congress was eager to have all the states surrender their western lands and create a national domain for public land sales. Ultimately, in 1784, Virginia ceded her northwest territories but not until Mason kept Madison and other congressmen informed about the background of various claims; and his influence was so great that the Ohio Company's interests were always protected.

Sometime during the winter of 1779-1780, Mason received the account of George Rogers Clark's conquest of the Illinois country, and this good news came at the right moment. Clark's daring raids sealed the validity of Virginia claims in the west, and slammed the door on the rival Vandalia Company that had troubled Mason for years. Besides all that, the 75-page letter was vastly entertaining. We can only speculate, but what a winter's night entertainment the children at Gunston Hall had if their father read them portions of Clark's hair-raising story of British and Indian intrigue.

In February 1780 Mason complained that the weather was chilly and "I find cold Sheets extreamly disagreeable"—although there must have been copper warming pans by all the fireplaces. Spring came with all kinds of good signs on the home front—the mockingbirds kept the woods on Mason Neck full of happy notes and the rains portended a good crop. In April Mason married an agreeable spinster—Sarah Brent—who became his companion and dear friend for the remainder of his life, and then he went to Richmond and battled for laws to keep the state solvent and the soldiers fed. He was disappointed in the Franco-American alliance—the whole thing seemed to be working out badly—and Mason wondered if the French were really giving a full effort. The worst news came from Camden, South Carolina, where the British won a smashing victory that exposed the Southern border of Virginia. Cornwallis appeared to have the Americans on the run and it would not be too many months before the treasonous General Benedict Arnold's raiders easily moved on Richmond and laid waste a part of the new capital.

The British decision to concentrate on the South stemmed from an incorrect premise—that thousands of southern loyalists would rise to greet the royal armies. Washington despised these "pests of society" but Mason was isolated from active loyalists and actually took pity on British-born subjects caught in the war's maelstrom with no desire to offend either side. On occasion Mason pleaded for leniency toward the innocent victims of the war who had lost much property and suffered other hardships mainly because they were in the wrong place at the wrong time. Unlike some planters, who considered merchants sharpers trying to cheat them, Mason looked upon the mercantile trade with a benign eye.

A champion of human rights in most instances, Mason also regarded property rights as sacred, and any merchant who conducted himself properly could expect Mason's sympathy. Mason hoped the French alliance would stimulate European trade with the United States and to help that end he placed large orders with Amsterdam merchants. In the late fall of 1780, before the Arnold expedition came from New York to Portsmouth, —Mason kept watch for the ship *Washington*, which left the Dutch port with an enormous cargo for Gunston Hall that included 13 scythes, "72 Quart Bottles filled with good french Brandy," and "29 mingles best Holland Gin" and came to £3,263—a princely inventory indeed.

William Mason prevailed on his father that fall to allow him to go south with the volunteer company raised in Fairfax County after the Camden disaster. Mason wrote Governor Jefferson, asking him to see that his son's outfit had good weapons as they moved toward the enemy. "It is a most discouraging Circumstance to a young-fellow to lead Men into Action, without proper Arms; and I fear the former

Regiments of Militia, serving to the Southward, have thrown away & lost so many of their Arms, that they can have little Dependence in being properly supplyed, on their Arrival at Hill's borough." In at least one regard, the county lieutenant had been lucky. "The late Draught, for the regular Service, has been not only quietly, but chearfully executed in this, & the neighbouring Countys," he reported. "I understand the Draft has been resisted, & prevented in some of the lower Countys, & some Lives lost; which I am not at all surprized at. If such dangerous Mutinies are not affectually quelled, & the Ring-leaders punished, our Government can't subsist."

Ill health kept Mason from serving in the House of Delegates at the October 1780 session, and he was sorry for the absence, particularly because the General Assembly would be choosing Jefferson's successor as governor, and Mason had reservations about their likely choice. As it developed, however, Jefferson's successor was Thomas Nelson, Jr., a good man and ardent patriot, and Jefferson was left a private citizen again for a while. To his mountain-top retreat in Albemarle County, Jefferson carried the peach tree seeds Mason had sent by his son. "Almost all my Portugal peaches were stolen this year, before they were ripe," Mason explained, "but I saved the few Stones I send you myself, & know they are the true Sort."

Mason hobbled around Gunston Hall and played host to General Nathanael Greene, who came bearing Washington's greetings and news "of our present distresses, and future prospects." Washington sent Greene with a note that worked on Mason's prejudices regarding regular forces. "We must have a permanent force, not a force that is constantly fluctuating and sliding from under us as a pedestal of Ice would do from a Statue in a summer's day," Washington warned. Relying on short-term enlistments and the militia had involved the country "in expence that baffles all calculation—an expence which no funds are equal to." Washington knew Mason's biases all too well, so he hit upon the one factor that would galvanize Mason into action on behalf of a regular force—the high cost of an amateur army.

Benedict Arnold's sweep up the James River to Petersburg early in 1781 caught Virginians by surprize. Tobacco warehouses and other public buildings were burned as the former American general served his new masters with energy, if not honor. Mason heard that Arnold was preparing a fleet of boats for raiding Potomac tobacco warehouses and wrote the Virginia delegates at Congress soliciting aid. George III and his advisors, Mason said, "are now acting upon

Principles of Revenge, determined to desolate what they despair of recovering . . . it is surely the Duty of the great Council of American to endeavour, if possible, to prevent the Mischief, and save from Ruin such Numbers of their Citizens," Mason urged.

Mason's suggestion was that a war damage fund be created to reimburse citizens whose property was destroyed by the British raiders, with the cost ultimately to be paid from "Dutys to be imposed upon all Imports from Great Britain . . . after a Peace, & to be continued until full Reparation shall be accordingly made." Mason thought this plan "wou'd at least be a Peice of Justice." He had hardly finished writing the letter when a British squadron worked its way up the Potomac within sight of Gunston Hall. "They have burn'd & plundered several houses, & carryed off a great many Slaves; tho' I have hitherto been fortunate enough to lose no Part of my Property," Mason added in a postscript.

Mason's good luck held out. The British paid a courtesy call at Mount Vernon but spared Washington's home and seemed determined to show how the rules of war could be observed despite the obvious temptation. Lafayette was in Alexandria on April 23 and reported to Washington that some slaves had left Mount Vernon with the British and Lund Washington had taken food to the British aboard their ship, hoping to have the blacks returned. Washington could not suppress either his anger or his sense of relief. He was glad the house had not been burned, but "to go on board their vessels; carry them refreshments; commune with a parcel of plundering scoundrels, and request a favor . . . was exceedingly ill-judged," the general told his cousin.

Dark as the situation seemed, Mason had more reason for optimism than he imagined. In his letter to the congressmen, Mason had expressed concern over the French intentions. "If our Allies had a superior Fleet here, I shou'd have very little Doubt of a favourable Issue to the War; but without it, I fear we are deceiving both them & ourselves, in expecting we shall be able to keep our People much longer firm, in so unequal an Opposition to Great Britain." What Mason did not know, of course, was that a trap was being set for Cornwallis by the British general himself—and a superior French fleet would spring the catch within six months of Mason's despairing letter. As military activity in Virginia increased, Mason grew impatient with military commissary officers who impounded food and forage with what Mason regarded as "much Confusion & Oppression."

At the end of May 1781 Mason briefly took flight from Gunston Hall and moved his family across the Potomac for safekeeping at his son's Mattawoman plantation. Panic gripped men who in better times had acted with calm, but a few days later Mason was back at home writing a leisurely letter to his son (still in France), while explaining that because of threatened raids "We have removed our Furniture, backwards & forwards, two or three times, upon different Alarms, by which it is very much damaged." Except for scratched chairs and wobbly table legs, however, the Masons had come off well. As the father reported, the family was "all well, except myself, who am but just recovering from a Fit of the Gout."

Mason also sent his son in France a second letter intended for the hands of Benjamin Franklin. In that message he candidly spoke of public uneasiness over the Franco-American military alliance. "The Bulk of the People here are staunch Whigs, strongly attached to the American Cause and well affected to the French Alliance," Mason wrote, "Yet they grow uneasy & restless, and begin to think that our Allies are spinning out the War in order to weaken America, as well as great Britain, and thereby leave us at the End of it, as dependent as possible upon themselves." Young Mason later told his father that the letter had been handed by Franklin to Count de Vergennes, the French foreign minister, but by that time the issue had already been settled.

DeGrasse came up to the Chesapeake Bay capes as Washington and Rochambeau moved on Cornwallis from the north. Lafayette's small force harried the British for a time, and in October the American plans seemed blessed by Providence—for once, everything went according to order. Only a month and a day before Cornwallis surrendered Mason was concerned about selling four or five stacks of hay to the French cavalry for hard cash as they passed by on their way to Yorktown. Whether Mason sold the French "about twenty odd Tonns" of hay or had it left is uncertain, but he heard the news from Yorktown with great satisfaction. "I congratulate you on the late signal Success of our Arms," he wrote Robert Carter the next week, "which there is Reason to hope will lay the Foundation of a safe & lasting Peace."

Cornwallis's surrender all but wrapped up the shooting part of the Revolution, but at the time this was not realized. Mason wrote an indignant protest over the seizures of military commissary officers that winter, denouncing their methods "by which many poor Familys have been ruined." Indeed, Mason warned, the war was being fought to end oppression, not to establish it. "A Man can have no Security in his Property; or must be reduced to the fatal Necessity of punishing the Aggressor with his own Hand; as in a State without Laws, every Man has a Right to do . . . This Method therefore of supplying the Public-Wants by Seizures, is of all others, the most disgusting, unequal, oppressive, & unjust; being in Fact, only another Name for public-Robbery."

Mason also wanted the British prisoners captured at Yorktown to be fed and housed at the expense of the United States, not of Virginia alone, and if necessary he favored a scheme to permit the British POWs to buy food from Virginians "with their own, or the King of Great Britain's Money," so that a little cash could flow in the stagnant state economy.

To keep matters straight, Mason swore before a commissary agent that he had not been paid for seventy pounds of beefsteak provided for the troops' use. Without doubt, the claim was honored, along with four others Mason eventually redeemed at the state treasury. From Mason's standpoint, it was enough to serve on the committee of safety and have a son in the militia—no need to give food off one's table or hay from one's stable for the cause. To his orderly mind, the line between one's public duty and one's private property was a clear barrier to gifts of food or hay to French or American soldiers.

The vague scent of peace sent Mason's thoughts traveling back across the Blue Ridge to all the thousands of acres still nominally held by the Ohio Company and his own private investments as well. He sent a son out to the Kentucky country to look around, and wrote letters to other speculators to take a reading on business prospects. Early in January 1783 Mason wrote George, Jr., who was taking the mud baths at St. Amand, France with a suggestion that Benjamin Franklin—now a peace commissioner at Paris—would help the young Virginian find a safe passage home. He told his son not to worry about the money his European trip had cost so long as it was spent in search of good health and not "in Extravagance, Dissipation, or idle Parade."

What did concern Mason was that he calculated a loss of not "less than £10,000 Ster: by the War, in the Depreciation of Paper-Money, & the Loss of Profits of my Estate; but I think this a cheap Purchase of Liberty & Independence." "I thank God," Mason continued, "I have been able, by adopting Principles of strict Oeconomy & Frugality, to keep my principal, I mean my Country-Estate, unimpaired; I have suffered little by the Depredations of the Enemy." Now 58, Mason considered himself an old man in retirement who would not accept public office again, "yet my Anxiety for my Country, in these Times of Danger, makes me sometimes dabble a little in Politicks, & keep up a Correspondence with some Men upon the public Stage."

Indeed, Mason worked to maintain his friendship with Washington, and asked the general to give sanctuary to Lawrence Washington, Jr., a distant relative of the Mount Vernon squire who had killed a man in a gunfight over a lady's honor. "I own I can't help feeling, as a Man, and as a Father, for old Mr. Lawrence Washington; who is a very worthy Man, and is exceedingly distressed by this unhappy Accident." To Arthur Lee, Mason sent his thanks for the word of the preliminary peace treaty and observed that although he had seen much public knavery and injustice motivated by "partial, local, temporary Views"—"But I hope every thing from Peace."

When news of the final treaty terms reached Gunston Hall Mason applauded the skill of the American negotiators and wrote a series of letters to public men congratulating them upon "the Establishment of American Liberty & Independence. Happiness & Prosperity are now within our Reach." To Patrick Henry he was more expansive. "Whether our Independence shall prove a Blessing or a Curse, must depend upon our Own Wisdom or Folly, Virtue or Wickedness," Mason noted, "judging of the future from the Past, the Prospect is not promising." Mason was distressed by the comments upon the unpaid debts owed by Americans to English merchants from the pre-war days. "In Conversation upon this Subject, we sometimes hear a very absurd Question 'If we are now to pay the Debts due to British Merchants, what have we been fighting for all this while?' Surely not to avoid our just Debts, or cheat our Creditors; but to rescue our Country from the Oppression & Tyranny of the British Government, and to secure the Rights & Liberty of ourselves, & our Posterity."

To reinforce his indignation, Mason wrote a petition for Fairfax County voters to sign in which they instructed their delegates in the General Assembly to work for fulfillment of American contracts with British merchants "adjusted to a legal scale of depreciation." Now that peace reigned, Mason's petition added, it was also proper that the Articles of Confederation be followed with great strictness. All local matters should be left to the states for their jurisdiction and guidance, and no general national tax should be approved for although the proposed customs "duties may be proper . . . [but] the separate States only can safely have *the power of levying taxes.*" Surely no voters ever had a more vigilant protector of their tax money than George Mason.

* * * * *

Peace brought problems, but they were the worrisome difficulties of a new nation, created from raw materials unlike any in world history. Mason almost stuck to his pledge not to reenter public life, but he was enticed out of retirement long enough to serve at the Federal Convention of 1787, where he made signal contributions to the proposed federal constitution before he refused to sign it. In the battle to ratify the convention's handiwork, Mason's essay that led off with the unanswerable point—"There is no Declaration of Rights"— created the conditions needed to bring on ten amendments by December 1791. After Madison and Jefferson worked to make the new government were republican, Mason admitted that after a few more changes "I could chearfully put my hand & heart to the new government."

When he was chosen a senator from Virginia, however, Mason declined the honor, not on political grounds, but because of ill health. Disabled by another "severe fit of Gout . . . with frequent Relapses," Mason said, "I can't reconcile myself to the Idea of receiving the Publick's Money for Nothing." During his last years, Mason enjoyed frequent visits by Madison and Jefferson, but was probably dismayed by Washington's coolness after 1789. The old neighbor heard and a rumor that Mason had intimated Washington had paid old pre-war debts in near-worthless paper money. True or not, the rumor hurt Washington and needlessly broke off a friendship that had lasted through two wars and a struggle for peace. How Mason felt about the rupture in their friendship is not recorded.

The record left is that of a man who contributed mightily to the winning of the War for Independence. Mason must have looked with some satisfaction at the Virginia state seal, with its triumphant Amazon of liberty standing astride the fallen tyrant and above the motto, "Sic semper tyrannis." He had helped design the seal which, in a symbolic sense, represented the prolonged struggle of the colonies from 1765 onward. In the most difficult times, Mason had been a leading force for elevation the Revolution to a higher purpose. Since 1776 men in every corner of the globe have harkened to his words as they too sought those rights "of Life and Liberty, with the Means of acquiring and possessing Property, and pursueing and obtaining

Happiness and Safety." Mason's own words summed up the whole of the Revolutionary experience:

> God has been pleased to bless our Endeavors, in a Just Cause, with Remarkable Success. To us upon the Spot, who have seen Step by Step, the progress of this great Contest, who know the defenceless State of America in the Beginning, & the numberless Difficultys we have had to struggle with, taking a restrospective view of what is passed, we seem to have been treading upon enchanted Ground.

A Note on the Sources

MOST of the material used in writing *George Mason and the War for Independence* was gathered from the George Mason Papers in the Library of Congress, Virginia State Library, Virginia State Historical Society, and University of Virginia. These are published in the author's edition of *The Papers of George Mason* (3 vols.: Chapel Hill, N.C., 1970). Other sources include Edmund S. and Helen M. Morgan, *The Stamp Act Crisis* (Chapel Hill, 1953); Samuel E. Morison, *Sources and Documents Illustrating the American Revolution 1764-1788* (Oxford, 1948); Don Higginbotham, *The War of American Independence* (New York, 1971); Paul H. Smith, *Loyalists and Redcoats* (Chapel Hill, 1965); Bernard Bailyn, ed., *Pamphlets of the American Revolution 1750-1776* (vol. I to date; Cambridge, Mass., 1965); and Curtis P. Nettels, *The Roots of American Civilization* (New York, 1939).